The Mumbai Midway

The Mumbai Midway

A portrayal & the portraits of the
middle class area of Mumbai

Pradeep C. Kirtikar

PARTRIDGE
A Penguin Company

Partridge books may be ordered through booksellers or by contacting:

Partridge India
Penguin Books India Pvt.Ltd
11, Community Centre, Panchsheel Park, New Delhi 110017
India
www.partridgepublishing.com
Phone: 000.800.10062.62

CONTENTS

PART - 1

A PORTRAYAL

PART - 2

THE PORTRAITS

THE MUMBAI MIDWAY

". . . . *A way of life in Mumbai by Middle class people has been depicted in this book. It gives a detailed account of the various facets say social, financial, political, and psychological of the life of the class that is the backbone of the society and without which the rich and poor classes would not have the meaning provided to them about their own survival. This particular class in India and especially in Mumbai has not yet been vividly sketched in English language. The book will attract those who show delight in knowing about the social structure of Mumbai, livings in metropolis of India, history of Mumbai, and those who want to revive the memories of the life they lived, or they were surrounded by. An articulate and witty commentary on the middle class of Mumbai . . . .*"

ACKNOWLEDGEMENT

Firstly, I am grateful to my son, Rugved, who, since he started staying in London 7 years since, has always been on the lookout for finding some or other resources convenient for the access to the English literature. He, despite my not being so eager, on his own sent me the e-book reader by means of which I could see a lot of English literature, for which, in fact, I was longing for, but which, before, was available for reading only on a piecemeal basis. For the publication of the present book, he has put a lot of effort in contacting and interacting with the required agencies.

My wife, Vinda, supported me a lot and helped to save my soul upright, which an initial writer requires the most.

My brothers, unknowingly to them, helped to keep the memories and passion about the earlier life existing in the mind, through the topics conversed whenever the coming together was occasioned.

Many friends pursued me with the praises, for which I do not know how honest I have been, and coaxed for writing.

I am grateful to all of them. My feelings are true and from the heart

Pradeep C. Kirtikar
Mumbai,
30th July 2013

INTRODUCTION

Having had a chance to spend years of childhood in the area that was, and instead is, predominantly middle class area of Mumbai, a great metropolis of the world, it was dwelling in my mind for quite a sometime that such useful observation, which I was exposed to, should not go waste without having put in the words, and presented to the world for feeling the life that is different, but not prominently accounted for as yet.

The book has been clearly divided into two parts, the first part describing the surrounding in which the characters depicted in the second part stayed or are staying. The first part elucidates the various aspects of the way of life of people in Girgaon, where the middle class inhabitants of Mumbai have been staying intensely; this first part itself is a captivating work that presents the aspects of life there in a striking manner. The first part provides for the insight of the flow of life in which the characters in the second part had their life spent.

Our family, comprising father—mother—my—my brothers, had an opportunity to stay in the area of Girgaon, and we the children of our parents passed the most part of our early days there, though our living accommodation was singularly different from the characteristically typical houses there. We could feel and enjoy the culture and surroundings of Girgaon, and for which we did not have to get entangled in life there on a day to day or say a minute to minute basis. The bird's eye view, for which I was subjected to, of life around gave an inclination to write, unknowingly and in the back of mind, the singular aspects of proximate atmosphere, and traits of the characters living therein.

The people of Girgaon, who of course largely belonged to middle class of the society, was exhilarated by themselves, they never repented or sulked for having them deprived of luxury and financial happy place that the higher and richer class was enjoying; their subordinate position, in comparison to that of the privileged upper class of the society and their not so fortunate position, did not bother them in a large scale so as to frustrate their constant effort at rising higher in the life; they sought for elementary form of life without harbouring hatred toward their current situation, on the contrary they were found to be taking maximum pleasure and enjoyment out of their current situation, so much so that others were inclined to regard their that position as their complacency. Their positive attitudinal way toward their current situation and the atmosphere was their beliefs that made them agree to stand current position and aim for better. They lived in dingy rooms, with ever increasing family, celebrating each and every occasion with such a frenzy that the wealthy upper class people would come to such a pass that they would appear to envy them and, sometimes, sulk by the soul for having deprived of such condition that they could not enjoy the life that the middle class of Girgaon was enjoying. They, the middle class, were never majorly overtaken by the financial worries that they were consistently exposed to, and any such problems never stopped them from enjoying the moments of life to the fullest, but within the means and sources easily available to them. The wealth and resources did not present to the fortunate class the ways of merriment that were available to the middle class; the ways available to the wealthy upper class were better as far as 'pomp and show' was concerned, but the joy and the buzz generated was bland in comparison to the lively delectation availed by the middle class out of their not fancy but enthusiastic celebrations.

The life of a middle class was easy, but certainly not dull, in contrast it was full of life; their problems of whatsoever nature also would affect their social life, because the concern shown by handy people, in such moments of problems, and over the course of several years of cohabitation, helped them to create, strengthen, and maintain the relations that were beyond the birth relations. And for a congenital condition of being like that they were not required to provide any additional efforts, for that condition used to take place effortlessly due to the near identical situation and congested cohabitation of them.

The characters depicted in the second part are right but not singularly similar to any living or deceased person because the traits that comprise each of the characters are a blending of several symbolic traits discovered in various real characters that lived or are living, in this middle class pocket in Mumbai that is Girgaon. I, therefore, consider myself fortunate to have saved from making a defensive cliché statement that, any resemblance of the characters with any living or deceased person is purely coincidental. Any reader who stayed or is staying in Girgaon will not be inclined to claim that he never have met or heard of the individuals sketched in this work, even though his efforts of identifying them with any of the persons that he knew from the area of Girgaon will cause him only to estimate. Though the characters have been sketched in a slight humorous style, that was the requirement of the work for making it appealing, and there has been no intention of casting any aspersion on any character that anybody may try to conjecture.

I will be glad to receive your reflections on the work, which you are suggested to send to my e-mail address.

Pradeep C. Kirtikar

Mumbai, India.
Email address:—pradeep.kirtikar@rediffmail.com

THE MEANINGS OF THE MARATHI COMMON NOUNS USED IN THE WORK

Aai :—mother

Aaji :—grandmother

Ahar :—a meal

Aytas :—stanzas from Kurran

Baraf Golawala :—a supplier of balls of grated ice sprinkled with sweet syrup

Barke Sheth :—a wealthy boy or a son of a wealthy man

Batata Bhaji :—an oil fried potato slice coated with thin dough of gram flour

Batata Wada :—a deep fried small ball of boiled potatoes coated with thin dough of gram flour

Bechanwala :—one who handles the sale in the illegal booze joint

Bhaji Galli :—a lane where vegetable vendors sit in the business

Bhajni Mandal :—a group singing religious, devotional songs

Bhatji :—a Hindu Brahmin that performs rituals

Bhojanalaya :—an eatery

Bhuvan :—a mansion

Bidi :—tobacco filled, folded, dry leaf for the purpose of smoking

Brun Maska :—soft bread with butter applied in it

Bun Maska :—sweetish, soft bread with butter applied in it

Chalwal :—a movement

Champi Malishwala :—a masseur

Chapati :—a flattened wheat dough baked on hot griddle

Chappal :—sandals of natural form

Chawl :—a tenement

Chhakka :—a womanish man

Chicken Masala :—thick gravy containing chicken pieces

Chivda :—a mixture of fried ground nuts, coconut slices, and beaten rice added with condiments

Chowpaty :—an area of sea shore

Chutney :—a crushed mixture of likes of chilli, coconut, coriander, and so on

Daal :—soup of pulses

Dada :—a chief of the miscreants from the lane

Dalimbi :—sweetish curry of peeled beans

Dholki :—a small drum

Dhotar :—a thin, long cloth worn systematically to serve the purpose of leg wear

Egg Masala :—thick gravy containing pieces of boiled eggs

Gada :—a game played with the unused rim of the bicycle and a staff

Gajra :—a small garland of fragrant flowers meant for wearing in hairdo

Ganderi :—sugarcane—peeled and made into pieces

Ganderiwala :—a seller of ganderis

Ghungru :—small bells

Girgaonkar :—a resident of Girgaon

Gola :—a medium ball

Goonda :—a ruffian

Gulab Jamun :—refined butter (ghee) fried small balls of dough of combination of refined flour(maida) and condensed milk immersed in sugar syrup)

Haldi Kunku :—literally turmeric powder and vermillion, but referred to celebration of women

Havaldar :—a police constable

Hijda : a eunuch

Hututu :—an outdoor game played between two teams of seven members each

Idli :—a vapoury boiled flattened balls of rice dough

Jayanti :—a posthumous birth anniversary

Kabaddi :—an outdoor game played between two teams of seven members each

Kandil :—a paper lantern

Khadi :—hand spun coarse cloth

Kheema :—minced mutton and a recipe of that

Kulfi :—home—made ice—cream made of thickened milk

Kulfiwala :—a seller of Kulfi

Lagori :—a game played with seven small pieces of tiles and a softball

Lenga :—a leg wear like pants but of thin cloth

Mandal :—a circle or group of people coming together with a common motto

Mandir :—a temple

Masala Dosa :—a griddle fried thin layer of soft rice dough

Maska :—butter

Matoshri :—a reverend mother

Mawali :—a miscreant

Medu Wada :—an oil fried flat ball of fermented dough of Vigna Mungo (Urad)

Missal :—a legume curry mixed with *chivda*

Mukadam :—a supervisor

Naman :—a devotional salutation

Navmi :—9th day of the Hindu fortnight

Niwas :—residence

Paan :—a betel leaf

Pagote :—a headgear made of a long piece of cloth

Paisa :—a coin valuing 100th part of a rupee, plural paise

Pandit :—a learned person

Pav :—a small bread

Pir :—a Muslim religious man

Piyush :—sweet buttermilk mixed with condiments

Pooja :—a ritualistic performance

Poornima :—a full moon day

Pugree :—a crimson coloured headgear of a vivid shape

Rangoli :—a temporary design made on the ground using marble dust and dry colours

Sabhagruh :—a hall where meetings take place

Sabudana Wada :—an oil fried ball of a combination of soaked sago and boiled potatoes and groundnuts

Sadra :—a wearing like a shirt

Sanyukta :—integrated

Shakha :—a branch

Sherbet :—a combination of grated ice, water, and sweet syrup

Shenga :—groundnuts boiled in salted water

Shengwala :—a seller of shengas

Sheth :—a moneyed man

Shrikhand :—water dripped out curd mixed with ground sugar and condiments

Tabla :—a pair of the tuned hand drums

Topi :—a cap

Vahini :—sister in law

Varkari :—a regular voyager of a religious place

Vassvalle :—fragrant

Vasudev :—a person visiting the areas after the dawn singing religious poems

Veni :—a small, tightly woven garland of fragrant flowers meant for wearing in hairdo

Wadi :—a hamlet

Zabba :—a wearing like an oversized shirt

PART - 1

A PORTRAYAL

THERE STAYS THE
MIDDLE CLASS OF MUMBAI

GIRGAON, THE MIDDLE CLASS MUMBAI

Before the independence, Mumbai was restricted from Fort to Dadar, and even Dadar was a sparsely populated area. The population of Mumbai, in those pre-independence days, was staying in the mixed way, spread all over the city, and no area was identified with any particular class of the population; the ruling British and some affluent Indians like the mill owners, the brokers, and the rulers of princely states had bungalows in areas like Malbar Hill and Cumballa Hill, which were considered as a rich class area; except the rich class area, all other areas were known as non-rich class areas or rather those areas were not identified with any particular class of the Indian population in Mumbai by that time, as classes in the Indians had not vividly emerged as yet. With the sense of freedom slowly overcoming the minds of Indians, many began coming to Mumbai for jobs or for starting the small businesses, with their small capital; the original residents of Mumbai began either to strive for higher education, for the purpose of establishing in rewarding professions and the important jobs, or to prepare for setting a new business and expanding the old one, which they had. By the mid of sixth decade, the people began settling in the areas, distinctly meant for the classes to which they belonged, which had emerged vividly in the 10 years after the independence; moreover, the inhabitation beyond Dadar, in the northern part of Mumbai, also had begun getting set by that time, providing the space for the newer and newer classes.

Many years since, before the independence, it was a boom period for the textile mills, and as a result of which the mills had been providing jobs for many in numbers. A flood of people had been coming from Konkan, and other regions of Maharashtra to Mumbai to join the mills as a worker; the jobs were plentiful in number and the pay was reasonably good, so many different aspirants kept on coming to join the mills, in addition to the existing workers finding jobs for their relatives. The mill workers preferred to stay in areas where their mills were located; the mills were mainly located in the central Mumbai, in areas like Parel, Lalbaug, Delile Road, Jacob Circle, Byculla, Eastern Worli, and in their nearby areas; hence those areas were predominantly inhabited by the mill workers and workers in the ancillary industries; naturally, the common population began knowing that area as the working class area. After the independence, the rich and influential Indians preferred staying, besides Malbar Hill and Cumballa Hill, in Church Gate, Worli Sea Face, Marine Drive, Nepean Sea Road, and Warden Road areas; those areas were necessarily considered as the higher class areas.

In those days, the land owning families were staying in places like Malad, Goregaon, Parle, Versova, Borivali, Mulund, Bhandup that their land was situated, they were residing in the big houses, with their servant families staying in the small houses around; besides the servants of the landowners, some poor families would stay, as tenants, in the rooms about the redundant houses of landlords; all those people, who was staying alongside landlord families, mostly belonged to the lower class or lower middle class.

The remaining class, which was undoubtedly considered to be middle class, concentrated mainly in the areas of Girgaon, Dadar and penetrated into adjacent areas like Mahim, Matunga, C. P. Tank, Gaodevi, and Kalbadevi. Dadar had the middle class dwelling in the comparatively small strip of land, on the western side of the railway station, between the railway track and the Shivaji Park, which was inhabited by the higher class, whereas Girgaon had the middle class dwelling in the sprawling, vast area on the eastern side of the Charni Road railway station; resultantly, the middle class dwelling in Girgaon was far bigger than that in Dadar. There was also a substantial difference between the two sets of middle class people respectively settled in Dadar and Girgaon, the difference was evident in the lifestyle and outlook of each of the sets. The middle class people in Dadar, ostensibly, had a perception that they had been entrapped in that class and that they should strive hard to get out of it as early as possible, whereas the middle class people in Girgaon had accepted its middle class status as their way of life, they were satisfied with the class that they had been placed, and they were enthusiastically putting all efforts to make their life more meaningful and joyful, by way of undertaking the constructive activities in the fields of dramatics, theatrics, music, politics and literature. The middle class in Girgaon had developed a sense of pride and identity about the middle class lifestyle, which had been established and followed there. From the 70s, the middle class slowly began shifting to the western and eastern suburbs of Mumbai, and in the present days the middle class can be said to have scattered all over the northern part of Mumbai. However, in the 60s, 70s, and 80s (and even in the present, to the most part), Girgaon was the area of Mumbai that genuinely represented the middle class inhabitants of Mumbai.

THE MIDDLE CLASS STATUS

The level of families in Girgaon is ranging between the lower middle class and the middle class; any family in Girgaon attaining higher class rank shall soon be on its way out of Girgaon in areas like Shivaji Park, Prabhadevi, Vile Parle, Juhu, and such other places; whereas, in case of lower class people, its failure, at an effort to reach the lower middle class status, will slowly push it off to Jogeshwari, Bhandup, Malad, and such places. The middle class of Girgaon consists of multiple layers, say from the lower middle class to the class that is on the threshold of a higher middle class; the people from the class, which is below or above the layers of middle class, shall be thinking, sooner or later, to say goodbye to Girgaon; with many young people leaving Girgaon for better living conditions, the general nature of Girgaon, however, has been tilting toward the lower middle class than the middle class.

THE GIRGAON CULTURE

Girgaon is not a geographically demarcated or an administratively defined area; it is a culturally identified area. Girgaon is recognized by its cultural uniqueness, which is exceedingly homogenous and striking in its character. The distinct facets of the Girgaon values are apparent in its style of language, social habits, schools, theatres, social and political views, and many other besides aspects. The basic character of Girgaon is a Maharashtrian, though many other people, from the different regions, have been staying there, having mingled with the culture of Girgaon and speaking the same language that the majority speaks, and becoming as nostalgic as any *Girgaonkar* shall get after leaving Girgaon.

THE NAMES OF THE LANES IN GIRGAON

Sometime back, in my rare visit to Girgaon, I happened to be at the mouth of Gai*wadi*. I had a friend with me, who had come with me to Girgaon with an aim to meet his relative, who had recently shifted to Girgaon and was staying as a paying guest in the house of an old lady. My friend was not from Mumbai and was visiting Girgaon for the first time. My friend, as he was confused with the bustle of the Girgaon road, was looking around and asking me various questions, as a child taken to the fair would do to his father. He suddenly asked me, what that place, where we were standing, was called, and I quickly answered him that, it was Gai*wadi*(Gai means a cow). His voice was teasing, out of an undeniable point which he seemed to have already pondered over, and in that note he said to me that, it appeared that the name of the area had been established by virtue of those two identical pieces of sculpture, by the head of a creature from the oxen family, installed there, but, he asked me, how one could say insistently that they were of a cow and not of a bull. I turned back and closely observed a pair of matching sculpture, which were mounted on a pair of stone pedestal, each placed on the either sides of the entrance of Gai*wadi*, with each part of long disused iron gate fitted to each one of them; I had been seeing the busts of cows since my childhood, but at the moment I scrutinized them with a renewed interest. I inspected the old busts with a great contemplation, for some moments, for the first time in my life, and in a flash the secret was revealed to me, and I exclaimed 'found out, found out' in a fashion that Archimedes had done in that famous incident. I told my friend to take a close look at the sculpture, and when he did so, I told him to, please, assume the artistry of the sculptor that how nicely he had poured the feminine features in that small piece of sculpture. He listened to me and also looked closely at the busts, and nodded in an acceptance of fact, and afterwards he did not say anything. I was happy to have saved the reputation of Girgaon from the passing of an indignant remark. He asked me also, looking in the opposite lane, as to what that lane was known as and I told him that it was called by the name 'Kandewadi' that raised his curiosity further, and before he could shoot a series of questions I told him the names of the lane on the right and left of the place where we were standing, which obviously were 'Ambewadi', 'Kelewadi', 'Borbhat Lane', 'Mugbhat Lane'. He asked me whether all the names of the areas in Girgaon were after the items grown from the ground that I said that, it was not the point, though many names were in that way there were so many other places which were named after either the early owners of the areas or after the caste of the people previously (and even at present) stayed there; in the proof of that I, off the hand, got him acquainted with names like 'Devkaran Nanji *wadi*', 'Bhai Jeevanji Lane', 'Gazder Street', 'Thakurdwar', 'Kshatriya *Niwas*', 'Kasar *Chawl*', 'Bhatt *Wadi*', besides 'Fanas *Wadi*' and 'Tad *Wadi*' named after the jackfruit and the palm respectively. I also told him that, many a lane has been renamed after the name of some or other person from the late history, but till the present time they have been popularly known and referred, even by the young generation, by their old names.

THE EXPANSE OF GIRGAON

The area opposite to the Metro Theatre is known as Dhobitalao, and Girgaon begins at the hands stretch from there, say from Chandan *Wadi*. The main street of Girgaon, that is now called 'Jagannath Shankarsheth' Road, was formerly known as 'Girgaon Road'; this road, long before had been called 'Palva Road'. Jagannath Shankarsheth Road, which is commonly known as J. S. Road, stretches from Dhobitalao to Opera House and further, but its central portion, which is from Dhobitalao to Opera House, goes through Girgaon. J. S. Road, going south to north from Dhobitalao to Opera House, is intersected by one east-west road at Thakurdwar that a junction known as the Thakurdwar Junction is formed; this east-west road comes from C. P. Tank in the east and in the west it meets Queen's Road, which runs parallel to the eastern side of the railway line between Charni Road and Church Gate stations. One more junction is similarly formed at Prarthana Samaj by the east-west road coming from Grant Road on the east and meeting Queen's Road in the west; incidentally, Queen's Road runs parallel to J.S.Road. The area of Girgaon, as can be said, is the lanes on both sides of the J. S. Road from Chandan Wadi to Aryan High School and the lanes on both sides of the east-west road at Thakurdwar from Bhuleshwar to Queen's Road, and on the east-west road at Prarthana Samaj from Harkisandas Hospital to Queen's Road, and the lanes on both sides of V. P. Road from Ram Mohan School to Bhuleshwar. This is the area which is widely known as the main Girgaon or the middle Girgaon; however, the areas adjacent to this central area have some or other consequence of the culture of this main area, and those areas are Kalbadevi, Khet *Wadis*, Gaodevi, Lamington

Road, Tardeo, Opera House, and to some extent Crawford Market.

As far as main Girgaon is concerned the consisting lanes are Chandan *Wadi*, Sonapur Lane, Tad *Wadi*, Vijay *Wadi*, Shankar Bari Lane, Burrows Lane, Gangaram Khatrychi *Wadi*, Bhai Jeevanjee Lane, Hemraj *Wadi*, Devkaran Nanji *Wadi*, Karel *Wadi*, which lie on the western edge of the J. S. Road between Dhobitalao and Thakurdwar and on the eastern edge of the same part lie Zavba *Wadi*, Dhus *Wadi*, Nave *Wadi*, Ram *Wadi*, Vigas Street, and other small lanes. On the J. S. Road from Thakurdwar to Aryan High School on the left lie Sarkari Tabela, Mangal *Wadi*, Kele *Wadi*, Gai *Wadi* and other small lanes and on the right lie Mugbhat Lane, Borbhat Lane, Kande *Wadi*, Nikadwari Lane, Khotachi *Wadi*, Ambe *Wadi*, Benham Lane and Bhat *Wadis* 1 and 2. On the road, going to the west from Thakurdwar junction, one comes across no lanes except the rear openings of Sarkari Tabela and Karel *Wadi*, and on the road going to the east from Thakurdwar up to Bhuleshwar there exist Mugbhat X Lane, Jitekar *Wadi*, Dhobi *Wadi*, Koli *Wadi*, Fanas *Wadi* on the either side of the road. On the road, going to the west from Prarthana Samaj junction to Queen's Road, on the left lie Goregaonkar Lane and Tara Baug and on the right lays only one lane which goes to Roxy Theatre and Opera House Theatre. On the road going to the east from Prarthana Samaj to Harkisandas Hospital, there are only tall buildings which lay on both sides of the road, except on the right side there exist Bhatwadekar *Wadi* and Kshatriya *Niwas*. In the middle of the road from Prarthana Samaj to Harkisandas Hospital, a road called V. P. Road intersects this road. On the east, from this intersection, V. P. Road goes to C. P. Tank and Bhuleshwar, on the left of V. P. Road lie Deshmukh Lane, Navalkar Lane, Dubhash

Lane, Sikka Nagar, and Wilson Street and on the right lie Khotachi *Wadi* (rear opening), Amrut *Wadi*, Sadanand *Wadi*, and Sadashiv Lane. The big road, near Harkisandas Hospital and going to the east to Gol Deool (Round Temple) and Null Bazar, was known as Girgaon Back Road of which on the right side there are back openings of the lanes on the left side of V. P. Road and on the left exist many Khet *Wadis*, this road is considered as an eastern outskirt of Girgaon. Besides the lanes, which are mentioned, there are many other small lanes and the by lanes in the intermediating area, which along with main lanes as described earlier indisputably constitute Girgaon.

THE LIFE IN GIRGAON

In the 60's and 70's, the life of people of Girgaon was easy and non-complex. The majority of the *Girgaonkars* belonged to a salaried working class, mainly in the jobs that could be called the white collared jobs, like the clerks in the private or government offices, the accountants in smaller offices and shops, the sales supervisors in the traditional shops; offices, shops, and other workplaces were located in the nearby areas such as Fort, V.T., Church Gate, Sewree, Grant Road, Worli, C. P. Tank, Paydhuni, and Dhobi Talao.

Those who went to the offices in areas like Fort, Church Gate, Byculla, and correspondingly little further areas, where from to come home for lunch was inconvenient and impractical, would be ready by 9.30 in the morning to leave for the work, having had their lunch well before 9 o'clock. They would leave home once a song programme on the radio stations—Mumbai A or Mumbai B—was over by 9.45, and reach a bus stop or railway station in five minutes, the bus or train ride would take another 7 to 10 minutes to get a railway station or a bus stop near the workplace, and from there they could be in the workplaces in another 5 minutes; they would reach their offices well before 10.15 that the working hours began in most of the offices. During the lunch time, they might eat some small snacks in the office canteens before whiling off the remaining time, in the nearby areas of the office, in the company of office colleagues. After office hours, they returned home about 5.30, had their tea at homes, and, after resting for half an hour, they would join the chit chatting groups in the common galleries. When the dinner was over by 9 o'clock, they would pull a *lenga* and a half sleeve *sadra* from the drying wires and wear those clothes, with the drying rumples still on them, and proceed to the *paan* stall, where the standing meeting of the regular members had been taking place every day. They would discuss every issue like cinema, politics, theatre, sport, business, states' economic policies, foreign policy, and their own office politics and so on, conveying to and forcing on each other their own views on subjects, as vehemently as possible, with indefatigable zest. It would be 10 o'clock, the time to return to their homes and switch on the radio stations that broadcast some popular programmes listened to by routine before going to sleep. It would not be more than 11 o'clock, when they retired to bed.

In the case of those, who had their workplaces at the walking distance from home, the routine of the daytime was slightly different. They were leaving their homes, by 9 o'clock, for their shops or other such type of establishments, without eating the lunch but eating only a light breakfast at home. They used to come home for lunch largely by 1 o'clock; after the lunch, they would have a nap of one hour or more before they leave again, by 3.30, for the workplace. They would return home by 8 o'clock and join the other members, after dinner at home, for a daily late evening practice.

On Sundays and holidays their plan would be like going to the markets, in the morning time, to get unusual veg or non-veg items for the holiday lunch, then attending to some work at home like going to the saloon, alone or with children, or calling the barber at home for a haircut; remaining time, till the lunch, would be whiled away reading the news-papers or chit chatting in the galleries. After having lunch, they would get a refreshing holiday nap in the afternoon, and in the evening they would take their families to *Chowpaty* or the homes of the relatives staying near. When they came back home, they would like to sleep earlier than usual, thinking about the cycle of routine beginning the next day.

On some Sundays, there would be a programme of going, taking along the family, to the place of some relative, staying at a distance place, for lunch. All family members would be done at 9.30 in the morning, after having taken the bath and wearing the clothes suited to visit a relative's house. The place of the relative, staying at Vile Parle, Bandra, Ghatkopar or such other places, would be reached well before 12 o'clock. The members of the families of the guest and the host would spend the time exchanging the pleasantries and touching the 'in-family' matters. Before long, the lunch would be taken together, only the wife of the host preferring to eat only after serving food to everybody. The food items in the lunch would be the same, what the guests would have had in their own home. What that required for refurbishing or strengthening the family bonds was an invitation to lunch at each other's place, it did not require any particular meals included in the lunch. After lunch, the male members of both parties would, perhaps, desire to go to the *paan* shop for having the *paan* there, and take few *paans* for the ladies at home. The guests would be proposed and insisted to have some nap, which everybody would feign having been taken till 4.30. Slowly, everybody would get up, the tea would be taken, and the guests would show a desire to get ready for the return journey. The host would urge the visitor to halt and start only after eating the dinner; the guest, however, would mildly turn down the idea, which, he knew, was customarily given and not to be considered seriously. The guest family would begin their journey back and reach Girgaon before 8.30; at home they would prefer to have a light dinner, before going to bed.

THE GUESTS AND VISITORS OF THE GIRGAONKARS

On some Sunday, a *Girgaonkar* would have his relatives family coming to lunch. He would be done by 10 o'clock, before which he would have gone to the market for essential purchases, overseen the wife bringing the house to a knick knack condition, seen to it that the children had taken a bath in time and worn neat dresses. After 10.30, some or other member of the family would be visiting the gallery of the house, every now and then, where from the approach of the guest family, upon their entering the lane, would be visible. Sometime after, a child of the house would recognize a guest family from the gallery and begin shouting excitedly; everybody in the host family would gather in the gallery for offering a welcoming smile, from the above, to the guest family. The guest family would be seen coming briskly toward the house of the host, with the wife and children grinning widely as they looked up to the hosts, and a man in the front, smiling as he looked straight in the lane, and glancing upward, intermittently. The rest of the programme of the day would be as similar as what a *Girgaonkar* family would come across on their Sunday luncheon visit to their relatives. Where ever the lunch might be taking place the host himself or his wife would not forget to mention that, how they were given the best mutton by the mutton Walla, the best chicken by the chicken Walla, and the best fish by the fishmongers, adding further that, though the relevant vendor was away on that day.

Besides the guests coming on Sundays for lunch and spending 5-6 hours at home, a *Girgaonkar* also had the guests coming to his home, for 5 to 30 minutes or so, in the form of the relatives staying nearby and usually meeting here and there in Girgaon, the friends of the head of the family, from the area or his office, the lady friends of the woman of the family, and children's friends, who would question the father or mother about his friends where about by calling him by a surname of the family and not by his first name, for example, if a surname of the family were Bapat a friend of the son would ask father whether Bapat was at home or where Bapat had gone, the older Bapat would then meet his question by giving him information about the junior Bapat; it appears strange in life that even the teachers are called by their first names like Ravi Sir, Vijay Sir, Janardan Sir, and so on. Other guests, who were mostly from the native places of the head of the family or his wife and who had some work in Mumbai, would come with preparedness that they would be accommodated for two or three days and not too. In Girgaon, it was difficult to find any guest staying with any family for a longer period, say a month or more, unless whom happened to be a brother or sister of the wife.

THE HOTELS IN GIRGAON

There were many 'Maharashtrian' vegetarian 'hotels' in Girgaon, each of which was famous for some or other Maharashtrian delicacy, though all the items in all the hotels were equally good in tastes. In fact, those hotels were the restaurants or the eating houses, but the people of Girgaon, by habit, used to call them the hotels, though the term 'hotel' conveys a different meaning. Each hotel was famous for a particular recipe, like 'Kulkarni Hotel' was well known for *batata bhaji* and *dalimbi*, 'Tambe Hotel' was known for *missal*, 'Velankar Hotel' was famous for *chivda* and *batata wada*, 'Vinay Hotel' was famous for *missal* and *batata wada*, 'Virkar Lunch Home' and 'Kona Hotel', facing Majestic Theatre, were known for the sumptuous, wholesome, and delicious meals, 'Prakash' on V. P. Road opposite Ganesh *Mandir*, though a tiny place, was crowded by the people for *piyush* and *sabudana wada*, 'Purohit'-'Sandu'-'Panshikar' were also noted for the same items for which 'Prakash' was. These vegetarian hotels were run by the Maharashtrian Brahmins; the territory of non-vegetarian 'Maharashtrian' food had been largely taken care of by the Bhandaris from the 'Konkan' region of Maharashtra and the hotels like 'Satkar' at Thakurdwar, 'Anantashram' in Khotachi *Wadi*, 'Dhanaji Mutton Plate House' near Girgaon Court, 'Samarth *Bhojanalaya*' in Borbhat Lane were particularly popular with the non-vegetarian population of Girgaon. Many times, the people from other parts of Mumbai, when they came to Girgaon for some purchasing or for meeting the relatives, would make it a point to visit these places of eating in any case. Many times, in the 60's and the 70's, the persons visiting the homes of relatives in Girgaon would, ostensibly, come with their stomach full and refuse to take any eatables at the house of host for an obvious reason that they would not reveal, however, to anybody. These hotels were frequently visited by many well-known people of that time, like the Marathi Dramas and Cinema artists and the Journalists, when they craved for the tastes that they had relished sometime in the past. 'Anantashram' in Khotachi *Wadi* was frequently visited by the members of the famous Kapoor family, like Shashi Kapoor, Randhir Kapoor, and Rishi Kapoor; Raj Kapoor, when alive, had been visiting the place on several occasions.

These hotels had their heyday in the 60's and the 70's, that time they were crowded with customers, and it was hard, especially in the peak hours, to get a place easily. Their business, however, began falling down by the end of the century, for many old timers had begun shifting to the suburbs, and the new generation had begun liking the new items of snacks, especially South Indian and North Indian varieties. The first such shock to the traditional hotels in Girgaon was given, in the late 60s, by 'Raja Refreshments', the south Indian restaurant. The young generation began crowding 'Raja Refreshments' for eating cutlets, tomato omelettes, besides traditional South Indian items like *masala dosa, medu wada,* and *idli.* 'Raman Hotel', opposite Aryan High School near Opera House, also gained a reputation, in the first 70's, for its steamed *idlis* and *dosas,* served with unusually delicious *chutney*; the hotel was run for some years, and it was successful in maintaining its popularity till the last, but the owner found out that selling the motor spare parts was more profitable a business than selling *idlis* and *dosas,* so he quickly changed the business that the *Girgaonkars* found a reason to get nostalgic, whenever they walked past the shop, which would have been thronged then by the bland customers of the spare parts.

Most of the hotels had the names after the surname of the owner, but the customers, for years together, would not know the person who that could be identified as the actual owner. The person sitting on the cash counter would seem to be a paid servant, though, he would seem to be more deferential than the true owner would have been, and he would not seem to be interested in establishing any interaction with customers; sometimes, some talkative customers, however, would manage to scrape acquaintance with him, they would be found calling him by his name, which would be different from the name of the hotel, meant to say from that of the owner. The majority of the customers, visiting the hotels in Girgaon, would keep their interest confined to satisfying their tongue and taste, such performance of their confining the interest would be in consonance with the expectation of the hotel owner and his servants; in the case of need, a customer would draw attention of any hotel staff by calling the name of the hotel, which would mean by calling the name of the owner. If a person were eating in the Mr. X hotel and he required a glass of water then he was attracting the attention of any staff member of the hotel by calling him by name Mr. X, at length, a glass of water was served by the servant without a sign of disapproval on his face.

The forbidding rules in hotels, in Girgaon, were not as severe as in their illustrious counterparts in Pune, the owners also were not as apathetic to customers as their brethren in Pune were, but a request for any other favour or a complaint about any food items would be met with only a casual glance, regarding the customer as if he were a strange person; as per their idea of the business, 'listening to the complaint is as good as redressing it', and their deep rooted conviction was that, 'the customers need us more than we need them'.

The rest of the servants in the hotel, except a cash counter person, would be of the farmhand families from the owner's village in the Konkan region of Maharashtra; they would spend their whole life in the service of a hotel owner chosen by them, going to the village, only for 15 days every year, on the eve of Ganapati or Holi festival. They were never seen out of the hotel, and they were also not seen giving any opportunity to anybody for developing a relationship with them as if it was one of the service conditions of their job; they were, however, presenting themselves to customers with an indifferent gentleness and they were not being susceptible to manhandling the customers as it is there, in the present, in some of the hotels owned by people from out of Maharashtra. They would be seen performing their allotted duties in the hotel, for years together, till the time they found themselves incapable of carrying on any further. In 'Kulkarni Hotel', as per what that was heard, there was a servant, who had been doing nothing but spilling the beans for more than 25 years, his case would usually be given, jestingly, by my friend to anyone, who expressed outrage toward boredom and monotony in the present job.

Some hotels like 'Kona' and 'Virkar' were serving only meals, whereas some hotels, like 'Prakash', 'Panshikar', 'Sandu', 'Purohit', and 'Kulkarni', were serving only snacks. The other hotels served meals as well as snacks both. That was about vegetarian hotels, non-veg hotels served meals as well as snacks both.

There were many people in Girgaon who had no option but to eat in the hotels. They were people who were staying alone in Mumbai because their family was left behind in their native place for some difficulty, or they were widowers or not married till late age and staying with a brother's family only for shelter, or they were young men staying as a paying guest in the houses of the old ladies; all those people had to depend on the hotels for their needs of food throughout the day, from the morning tea to the dinner. The hotels, which served only snacks and refreshments, would have customers coming to them throughout the day from 9 o' clocks in the morning to 9 o' clocks in the night, they would have a stable business throughout the day, but their business, however, would be brisk in the evening. The hotels, which served only the meals, would have customers from 11 to 2 in the afternoon and 7 to 10 in the night. The hotels which served meals and snacks both, and the hotels which served only the meals would remain closed, from 3 to 5 in the noon, for the purpose of rest hours to the staff, and cleaning the place and vessels. All the hotels used to have a brisk business in the first week of the month that pay days fell, thereafter, the business collections would be waning as the days passed till the time next pay days arrived.

In those days, the hotels were found to be visited only by the men; the ladies rarely accompanied a man to the hotel, except when there was a reason to go to the quality meals restaurants like 'Virkar' and 'Kona'. The frequent visitors to the hotels would be the sole men as described earlier, as well as the married men, who would visit hotels despite delicious food available at home. The married men would visit the hotel when they craved for a particular food item, they would usually visit the hotels single, but on some days, chiefly in the first week of the month, the children might be accompanying them. That time, the ladies were just deprived of any particular, specific food available in the hotels because firstly there was no practice of taking ladies to hotels, and secondly the system of 'home delivery' or 'take away food' had not set in yet; the men were enjoying the privilege of relishing the tastiest food available in the hotels as well as at home.

The non-veg hotels generally had an identical routine as what the veg hotels had, except that the owner was required to possess a strong mind in order to deal with the customers visiting the hotels in an inebriated condition.

It is learnt that many 'hotels' have since been closed or leased out by the original owners; if a few are still being run, they are found to be bereft of their former glory.

THE CRAZE OF DRAMAS IN GIRGAON

Besides going to the hotels the other favourite 'pass time' of a *Girgaonkar* was that of going to the Marathi dramas or stage plays, mainly at the 'Sahitya Sangha *Mandir*' in Kele*wadi* and some time at distant drama theatres like 'Rang Bhavan' at Dhobitalao, 'Damodar' at Parel, 'Shivaji *Mandir*' at Dadar, 'Birla *Matoshri Sabhagruha*' at Church Gate, and 'Shanmuganand' at Matunga. The people of Girgaon of that time were prepared to do anything in the name of drama, after a style of a crazy person doing anything in the satiation of his craving. They discussed, in the balconies-trains-offices, each and every drama running or soon coming on the stage; they searched the newspapers, as soon as they arrived in the morning, for the dates of the plays and for the dates of the opening of booking plan; they patiently stood in the long queue for several hours in the morning to get the tickets, before proceeding to their workplaces and regretting boastfully to the bosses for a late coming; they bunked their offices in case the bosses were harsh and difficult to manage, or the tickets got after an unusually long time, making it difficult to reach the office in an agreeable time; they came early from the offices so they could start on time and reach the distant theatres, situated as far as at Parel, Dadar and Matunga; they accommodated their equally drama crazy relatives, coming to watch late night unique plays in Girgaon from some places in the suburbs, for a night in their small rooms; they forced same toleration on their relatives staying in the far off areas, where existed visitable drama theatres, and where rare play was to have taken place; they stuck their ears to the radios, with an erratic frequency, for 3-3 hours in order to listen to the broadcast of some famous dramas; besides theatres they thronged every lane and street, during the Ganapati time, where the plays were performed by the drama companies from Parel, Lalbaug or likewise working class areas; they visited Bombay Book Depot to buy the drama books for sending to their relatives in the villages, who were eager to prove their acting talent before the local population. What have they not done, in those glorious days of dramatic activities of the late 50's and the 60's and 70's, for and in the subject of drama or theatrical performance? That is a question, whose answer cannot be found without a deep study. Certainly, they did everything what they could not do.

AN EVENING OUT OF A
HAND TO MOUTH FAMILY

A hand to mouth family from Girgaon of the 60's and the70's would take to some enjoyment on some days in the year, by way of going to the theatre for watching the drama or any other stage performance, or the cinema hall for watching the Marathi or Hindi motion pictures, or some modest hotel for relishing the vegetarian or non-vegetarian food. On some happy occasion, there used to be a combined plan that of like going to the theatre or cinema hall was preceded by a dinner at a moderate hotel of choice. The head of the family, a husband, would come early at 4.30 or 5 p.m., from the work, by availing explicit permission that might have been got approved well in advance; as soon as he came, the preparation for being ready for the revelation was begun in the family; firstly the mother would be going from 'a place to place' in the *Chawl* for finding out the children, from where they were, and warning them to get home at the earliest in order to get done in time. At length, the children would gather at home and hustle bustle of getting ready would begin; the husband would get ready at the last, meantime availing him a rest either sitting in the chair or lying on the cot. By 6.30 or 7, they would begin their fabulous evening sojourn and firstly head toward the hotel chosen well in advance, the leisurely walk to the hotel would not take more than 15 minutes. Once in the hotel and conveniently seated they would look forward to placing an amicable order; the placing of an order would not be a problem because the menus that time were not as cumbersome as they are these days; mostly the fixed meal would be ordered with an extra sweet item like *Shrikhand* or *Gulab Jamun*. The dinner would take half an hour or so to finish, thereafter, the family would continue to 'Sahitya Sangha Mandir' for watching the play or to 'Majestic' or 'Central' Cinema Hall for watching the films show, the economy class tickets of the show would have been booked on an earlier day. They would regulate themselves in the crowd outside the hall, waiting to rush in as soon as the doors of a hall were opened. They would rush into the hall, along with the crowd, as soon it was allowed; after initial confusion and the slight arguments they would settle in their proper seats, however, with a heart palpitating, at least for the first half an hour, at every nearby appearance of the torch bearing door keeper, lest he should declare that they occupied the wrong seats. Soon the show would begin, and they would become a fear free and start enjoying the show. At length, the interval would come, and a husband would inquire with a wife whether she would like to go out for having the snacks that she would reveal her denial and strike at having an idea of spending on any food item, so soon after having dinner just less than two hours before. The children, however, would not budge and follow the father under a pretext of nature's call. The father would go out with the children, take them to a crowded toilet, where they would oblige to nature's call. After that, he would hang around the snack stall from the distant, grabbing the hands of children with each of his hands; the children would not settle for less than a Samoa each, so he would buy two small butter paper bags containing two Samosas each and everybody would eat one each Samosa on the spot while the husband holding one bag containing one Samosa for taking in the hall for the purpose of a wife. They soon would come into the hall and resettle in their chairs, with a minor realignment after the obstinate wishes of the children. The husband would push, as softly as possible, the bag containing Samosa in the hand of wife that she would utter some words of calm reproach but soon start eating the Samosa slowly, as far as possible avoiding the crumpling noise of the butter paper. The show would restart and, at length, end. The family slowly would pull the feet out of the hall with the crowd and, soon, part way with the dispersing crowd, they would start walking toward home; it would not take more than the 10 minutes to get home. The silence would reign till they reached home; the children would be already tired, on reaching home, the children, on the insistence of the parents, would hesitatingly wash their feet and hands and go to sleep as swiftly as possible. At length, the wife would, lovingly, tell the husband, 'I genuinely enjoyed today evening', and ask him, 'how much did you have to spend?' the husband would respond, 'Don't worry, not more than nine rupees, and it will not appear, in a way, of our intention to take you a sari next month'.

A WELL TO DO FAMILY'S EVENING OUT

In the 60's and the 70's, the head of the well to do middle class family, by the Girgaon standard, would take his family, once or twice a year, to 'Virkar *Ahar Bhuvan*' or 'Kona Restaurant' for enjoying the dinner. The day would be fixed as per the convenience of the head, and there was no need to have any particular occasion or any anniversary been celebrated on that day as the trend of celebrating the anniversaries was yet to appear in Girgaon of that time. The programme would be decided, and the word would spread well in advance, on the prescribed day the family would start by 7.30 in the evening for the joyful visit to the hotel; the meals would consist of the decided items of the hotel and there would not be any opportunity for the selection except a limited scope of the sweet items, the dinner would cost the head the whole twenty five rupees, which were sufficient for common people to eat 40 meals in a routine but decent hotel. The dinner programme might or might not be followed by the programme of going to the theatre to watch the drama or cinema show. For a few days, the description of the evening and food would be continually heard, from the children of a well to do family that had gone to enjoy the food.

THE GIRGAON CHOWPATY

Hardly anybody goes to *Chowpaty* in the morning time, except some students of the colleges, in the near vicinity, who go there, bunking the classes, along with friends, and some young boys, who go there cycling in the vacations. By afternoon, the traffic on the road disturbs a visitor more than what the serenity of the seashore refreshes him; also it is treacherous to walk, on the sand of the sea shore, under a scorching sun of an afternoon, you, therefore, will not find anybody there except also the college students, who come there, mostly with a sweetheart, to enjoy the peace within the slight bustle around. *Chowpaty* begins having some life by 4 o clock in the late afternoon, but it assumes a different and delighted look as the night begins falling. In a late evening or an early night, the sight of the neon signs visible from the distant spots in the otherwise bleak surroundings, an invigorating and salty breeze slowly coming from the sea, and a coldness of the massive sand bed send one into an ecstatic mood, and one forgets about the miseries, sorrows, problems of the present life, at least for some time; also, after leaving the area, the calmness and quietness prevails in one's mind for a sufficient long time what may extend into next few days. In the 60's and the 70's, *Chowpaty* had not been as crowded as it is these days. In those days, a person could come here alone, or with a friend, or with a sweetheart and gain an ecstatic and relaxed state of mind. For *Girgaonkar,* it was remarkably easy to reach *Chowpaty*, and it hardly was taking 10 minutes for him to get there from any place in Girgaon; the feet of any *Girgaonkar,* from a young boy to an old man, used to get to the sand bed or promenade of *Chowpaty*, in his leisure moments, at any reasonable time of the day or night.

It reminds me of Baa, who was an older lady of above 50 years of age, and who was our neighbour from the second floor of the building that we were staying. In the 60s, she used to get all willing, grown up children from the building to *Chowpaty*, in the late evenings of the post monsoon and the spring seasons, being in the months of October, November, February, and March. She used to gather the children, by 8.30 after their dinner at home was finished, and take them carefully to the sand bed at *Chowpaty*; after spending one hour there in playing and chit chatting and after the children were happy and refreshed, Baa would make them back home with more attention than that had been taken while going to *Chowpaty*, as the roads would have become more lonely and more quiet giving an indication of the approaching midnight. The memories of the late hours spent on *Chowpaty* must still be lingering in the hearts of many, who have shifted to another house several years since, and are now in their 60s.

THE IRANI HOTELS IN GIRGAON

Besides the regular 'hotels', Girgaon also had the 'hotels' with the different ambiance. They were the hotels (restaurants) owned by the Iranis ('in fact' the Iranians, but commonly known as Iranis in Mumbai), famously known as the Irani Hotels. Girgaon had the Irani Hotels situated in the obvious places such as Dhobitalao, Thakurdwar Junction, Prarthana Samaj Junction, opposite Central Cinema. The food items available in those hotels were different from what was served in other hotels; the Irani Hotels would sell *bun-maska*, *brun-maska*, cakes and other similar items besides tea, coffee and cold drinks. It always would confuse an ordinary man as to, who gave the Iranis such lofty places to sell the bread and butter, and what were they earning by selling such basic items, in addition to allowing customers for sitting in the hotel, for more than an hour, over a single cup of tea. They, however, had their way of business and that was evident in their erecting closed cubicles on one side of their extensive premises, providing privacy to couples who sought it; but in that case also they did not seem to have been making any substantial profit as they would charge only for the actual food and beverages consumed by the occupants of the cubicles, who were naturally inclined to consuming the time more than consuming the food, when such intimate enclosure was at their hand; perhaps Iranis were ardent followers of the notion 'seeing is believing' and they would not know unless they see with their own eyes as to what actually was happening behind the closed doors of the cubicles, the inside of which was out of sight for them for which their own doing was responsible. It was strange that they created in the hotel a closed place, where the occupants would become more involved in doing something else than giving a hand to the business of the hotel. The police were never seen bothering the Irani hotels, even though, they knew what that was happening behind the closed doors of the cubicles was not fitting in the definition of the legality, for which they could have caught the neck of the delinquents if that had happened somewhere else. Perhaps the police had faith in the formidable personalities of the Irani owners that they would handle a law and order problem, if arose, themselves instead of looking at the police for handling that.

By and large the Irani Hotel owners were reluctant to talk to anybody, especially to the customers. Their very appearance consisting of a fair but sagging face, tall and stocky body, massive forearms showing from the shabbily folded shirt sleeves, big stomach, fat palms, and short hair sticking in the head like a painted clay doll was sufficient to handle the customers and employees without uttering a word throughout the day; however, sometimes, a customer could see two-three Iranis gathering at the cash counter for talking to each other, in a style of the world leaders meeting at a luncheon on the eve of any international conference.

The kitchen of Irani hotel, by and large, would stand in the wasted corner of the huge premise of the hotel, it would have been demarcated with the help of a movable wooden partition; its looks would be similar to that of an uninvited guest, shrinking from the gathering at a party. The kitchen would contain no more than a sink, one cutting marble shelf, one or two knives for slicing breads, and one small stove with a tea kettle on it. A withered, weary face, every now and then running the eyes over the hotel from the small window of wooden partition, could be perceived to be a chef or cook of the hotel, whose duties were limited to making tea, filling cups, slicing bread, and applying butter to the bread slices; many times, waiters of the hotel would be seen performing, themselves, the duties of cook, without bothering him.

A waiter in an Irani hotel of that time was a point of immense curiosity that teased the minds of many customers of the hotels. Firstly it was not easy to identify him with any originality of whatsoever nature—geographic, linguistic, religious, or ethnic, and also his looks and manners would be substantially similar to that of a short time prisoner, who had been released on probation, on the basis of his assurance for moral behaviour. He would move about in the hotel in a civilian clothes that he apparently woke up in the morning, he would not have the uniform clothing for duties. Iranis were making their waiters look suspicious to the public eyes by way of a proclamation in writing, in no uncertain terms, that a currency note of a certain big denomination, hundred rupees at that time, should not be given to the waiters in payment of the bill. They also cautioned the customers, by writing on the wall, that the waiters were paid every day, suggesting thereby that any customer might not get a particular a waiter after that day, should he have any complaint later discovered about him.

As the years passed the Irani hotels gave in to the situation and began to implement changes in order to keep up with the time, they began selling items like beer, *kheema pav*, omelette *pav*, *chicken masala*, *egg masala*, in addition to what they were selling earlier, and sundry items like toothpastes, soaps, snack packets, wafers packets, and so on. As a result, the looks of the hotels changed than what they once had; the marble table tops were replaced by the laminated plywood tops, the cane chairs were replaced by the plastic chairs, and the cane tables were replaced by the commonly fabricated metal tables. The previous ambience of the Irani hotels, which prevailed in the British Raj time and many years afterwards, and for which the feet of people would turn to them, went behind the curtain of time. None of the Irani Hotels, except a few, have been closed down, but those which are being run, barring a few, are not the same what they were in the 60's and the 70's. There may not be an old *Girgaonkar* that does not have the memories of past Irani hotels lingering in his mind.

THE SEASONS IN GIRGAON

In the 60's and the 70's, the roads about Girgaon were made of tar; every road, whether it was a main road or a by-road or a road in the lanes, was a tar road. By the end of a summer season or in the beginning of a monsoon season the tar roads would have many small and large potholes about them, the public, in general, of that time would have no serious grievance about that condition of the road, because only the richest of rich used to own a car to run on the road and the common people had the clear footpaths to walk on. The monsoon used to come, more or less, by the 7th of June every year, and after starting sluggishness it would pick up, day by day, through the month of June, the month of July would see a heavy rain; it was said that *Pandit* Nehru had been in love with the scenario of a torrential downpour of Mumbai, and he used to spare a day or two, from his busy schedule of work, to come to Mumbai for enjoying torrential rain here.

After a heavy rain, the potholes were filled with water and turned into the puddles, the petrol dripping from some passing cars would mix with the water of puddles and create in them the rainbow hues, which were visible only if seen from the upper floor; when any child happened to look single-mindedly at the rainbow colours reflecting from the puddles, in the surrounding overcast sky, he was floated into a trance like state of mind and taken to an antithetic world.

The People would use the gum boots and a rain coat or an umbrella for going to work, the children would be happy if they were going to school, in the heavy rain, wearing a raincoat purchased new every year. Many employers used to provide their employees with umbrellas and sometimes even the gum boots if the nature of their work required such facilities. During the monsoon days, after coming home from the school and work, the children and their fathers used to stay only at home, either completing the studies or whiling the time away till the dinner was ready, the dinner would be served hot, and that would include the unique monsoon recipes. After dinner, before long, the beds would be made ready and everyone would slip quickly into bed pulling a cotton sheet over a body, for the climate would be rather chilled, and listening to the rattles of rain on the roofs of the nearby houses.

In the monsoon, the children in the lane used to play the games that were typically the monsoon games like *lagori* (played with seven small pieces of tiles and a softball), and *gada* (played with a disused rim of the bicycle and a staff). In the Hindu month of 'Shravana', which coincides generally with the month of August, the atmosphere would be a religious one, the programmes of *kirtan* (musical recital of the stanzas from religious books) were arranged in many prominent temples of Girgaon, which were attended by the elderly men, ladies, and the children accompanying them, those programmes used to begin by 8 0' clocks and end before 10 o'clock on the night; besides that, many religious ceremonies falling in that month were truly performed and celebrated in every home of Girgaon of that time. The monsoon season would be receding after the mid of August and would end by the second week of September; before that, in the meantime, the Ganapati festival would have come and gone.

The Indian season 'Sharad Rutu' (the post monsoon season) is supposed to begin by the mid of August and last till the mid of October. During that season the sky is clear, the nights are starry, and the weather is pleasant that the season is supposed to be a joyful and pleasant season and equated to the best Indian Season 'Vasant Rutu' (the spring). That time, the climate of Girgaon, in the season of 'Sharad Rutu', used to be absolutely enjoyable and joyous, the slight chilliness in the atmosphere could be felt in the open as well as within the houses, the piece of sky visible from some window of the room would be clear and full of many twinkling stars; the moonlight, sometime coming into the small room through a window in a particular position of the moon, used to be brighter and clearer than that was seen in the other seasons. Many famous and joyous festivals like 'Ganapati', 'Dussehara', and mostly 'Diwali', which are longed for and awaited throughout the year by everybody, fall in this season; the brightest and clearest full

Moon night of the year-'Kojagiri *Poornima*'—falls in the month of October. In the 60s, on the night of 'Kojagiri', the people of Girgaon used to organize a gathering in the moonlit terrace of their building, the people used to gather on the terrace from 9 o'clock, after having a light dinner at home, the cultural programmes of minor type were presented in the beginning by the boys and girls of the building, where after the light snacks, out of the contribution from every family, were served to everybody, a few dance and song items presented by the local talents used to entertain the crowd a lot; the programme would not exceeding last longer and would finish by 11.30; the atmosphere that the 'Kojagiri' programme was taking place was marked by a clear and starry sky, a pleasant moonlight, and an invigorating chilly weather, providing an indication of an approaching winter; the memories of the 'Kojagiri' nights, enjoyed in that the atmosphere, would not be wiped from the minds of the *Girgaonkars* forever. 'Diwali' comes after 'Kojagiri', and in those days the winter was felt by the time the 'Diwali' festival approached; the winter used to arrive early and stay for a longer period as there existed more open spaces in Mumbai than they do today, moreover, the population was not as thick as it is today. During that season, some families used to go out to visit the holy places or the hill stations as the Diwali holiday for schools was clearly falling in that season. During the mid-term holiday, popularly known as the Diwali vacation, the children would play cricket in the lane with a rubber ball, or by going to the grounds on Marine Drive for playing with the hard ball, they would play in the outfield of the ground, out of the mercy of the ground-man, without using any types of safety pads. In retrospect, the cricket played that way contributed more for demolishing than building the potential career of many aspiring cricketers from Girgaon of that time.

In those days, the winter was felt for four months, from the mid of October to the mid of February; the first and the last months of those four months were respectively the months of the waxing and the waning winter, and the period from the mid of November to the mid of January was perceivable to be a real winter season.

When the schools reopened after the Diwali vacation, there used to be a gap, at least of four months, in the festivities. In the winter, the people used to stay largely confined to their rooms, kept warm by shutting up the windows tight, they went to sleep earlier than that they did in the other seasons. Some street smart boys used to burn a bonfire on the nights of intense cold; the roads began to assume a deserted look well before midnight; an eerie silence, unlike in the other seasons, would prevail throughout the night and the sound of passing trains could be heard in the homes, due to the denseness of the atmosphere, at night time. On some winter evenings, the *hututu* matches were played in the lane; the match would be over before 10.30 as the night became chillier and chillier as the night hours advanced. The schools used to have the winter vacation, known as the Christmas' vacation, during the last week of December, the sporting events, of the schools and colleges, were taking place in an immediately preceding or succeeding week of the vacation, the picnics and trips of the schools and colleges were arranged mostly in January.

One notable festival, the 'Sankranti' festival, (a kite flying festival) falls in the mid of January; in the blowing wintry winds, the people of Girgaon used to gather on the terraces of the buildings or stand dangerously on the slanting tiled roofs of the buildings and fly the kites from 9 in the morning till 7 in the evening; again in the night, some enthusiasts would send the kites high in the sky with the small *kandils* (paper lanterns) tied to the string at each uniform space that would adorn the dark sky of a wintry night with hundreds of light lamps, the scenario in the sky used to provide an enormous pleasure to the eyes of beholders. The season, which prevails from the mid of October to the mid of December, is called 'Hemant Rutu' and the following season of two months, and ending in the mid of February, is called 'Shishir Rutu'. After the mid of February there begins the best season of the year that is called 'Vasant Rutu' and which prevails till the mid of April; in this season, the sky is clear, and the weather is lovely and friendly, the heat, however, will be ever rising as the days pass; in this season, in Girgaon, the flowers would bloom in the small gardens here and there and also in the pots hung in the galleries of the buildings. In Girgaon of that time, the prevalence of 'Vasant Rutu' (the spring) was perceivable on the visit to 'Bal-Bhavan' garden on the west side of Charni Road Station or 'Kamala Nehru Park' on Malbar Hill. The particular day festivals like 'Maha-Shivratri', 'Gudhi Padva', 'Ram *Navami*', 'Hanuman *Jayanti*', and 'Holi' fall in this season; in those days, these festivals were celebrated more systematically, sincerely, and ardently in Girgaon than they are done in the present. The festival of Holi falls in the beginning of 'Vasant Rutu' and that is traditionally celebrated by the people for expressing happiness for the arrival of that season. The celebration of the 'Holi' festival in Girgaon was more a social event than a family one, as the customary bonfires, of 'Holi', were burnt only on the streets, and the colouring festival, on the subsequent day, implying the application of colours to each other, was celebrated in the public places.

The latter half of 'Vasant Rutu' used to pass unnoticeable because the children, as well as the parents, somehow remained engaged in preparation for the final examinations of the schools and colleges; the examinations were over by the mid of April and the results of the school final examinations were handed out in the last week of April. The summer season, which equates the Indian season 'Grishma Rutu', begins in Mumbai by the mid of April and continues till the mid of June, though the people begin feeling the heat right from the turn of March. By the end of April, there were social celebrations in many lanes, the celebration would be over by the first week of May, and after that the buildings and lanes would appear betraying the desolate look, for many families would make for the native place for spending the holiday there till the schools reopened; the head of the family used to accompany the other members of the family to the native place and return to Girgaon, after a few days, for enjoying the bachelor's life of some days. The scorching sun and the oppressive humidity were keeping the people confined to the homes or offices during daytime, at which time the lanes and streets used to get more desolate, especially between 12 and 5 there would be remarkably few persons on the road. In the late evening, the people would go out of the house for strolling, in the open air, on the street or on the promenade of *Chowpaty* as it would be unacceptable, due to the high humidity and resultant sweating, to remain in the house. The time of going to bed would be shifted further at least by one hour than that in the winter and monsoon seasons; some people used to take to sleeping on the terrace or in the gallery, but the high humidity associated with the lack of provision of the fan, and the sun rising early in the morning were making their nights restless. By the end of May, the breezes from the south-west would appear and make some occasional solaces in the heat affected *Girgaonkars*, who would then begin awaiting the arrival of the monsoon and preparing to get ready for the rainy days; the unbearable heat and predictions about the arrival of the monsoon would become the topics of general conversation. In the turn of May, the people, who had gone to the villages, would start coming back to Girgaon, and that would dispel, day by day, the deserted look of the lanes and the buildings; the children, returned from the vacation, would swarm the book stalls for purchasing books for the new class, in view of the schools reopening on the 7th June. There would be drizzling by the end of the first week of June, which could be sensed as the beginning of 'Varsha Rutu'-the monsoon season; the new cycle of the seasons would start as it had begun a year before the year.

THE ATMOSPHERE IN GIRGAON OF THAT TIME

One, who is visiting Girgaon in these days, will find many buildings still standing at their places in more or less similar conditions that they were there 30 to 40 years ago, a few towers, built here and there, will only be the exception; he will find the same look in those buildings as it was there a few decades ago; the young residents of the buildings will still be found leaning over the railings of common galleries and looking into the road as they talked to each other; the tired old faces, noticed in the windows of their homes, will still be seen blankly looking at nothing in the street. A prima facie appearance of Girgaon is same as it was in the 60s and the 70s, but if an old *Girgaonkar* has a chance to observe and feel Girgaon for the 24 hours at a stretch, he will realize the changes that have taken place in Girgaon over a few decades.

THE SYSTEMS—SEWERAGE, GUTTERS, WATER SUPPLY

In those days, the streets and the lanes were systematically cleaned in the morning by the municipal workers, and on some days they were even washed clean with the water, in the early morning hour. The gutters were kept clean, and there had been no problem till then of the gutters getting choked. The passages and staircases of the buildings were swept every day by the sweeper, who was paid a monthly salary by the building owner. Sometime, the new owner of the building, on changing of the ownership, was seen taking a fancy to whitewashing the building that he had recently owned. The overall cleanliness was detectable in Girgaon of that time, the systems like sewerage, gutters and water supply had not begun to crumble till then; the water shortage, however, had begun being felt by the mid of the 60s and that persisted for few more years.

THE MODES OF TRANSPORT USED IN GIRGAON

It would not appear to the mind of any *Girgaonkar* to look for any mode of transport when he had to go as far as up to 2 to 3 kilometres of distance, in that case he used to, instinctively, get to the walking. For going to the places within 5 kilometres or so a *Girgaonkar* was using the bus service provided by the BEST, for going to the suburbs there was no suitable means other than the trains, which, at that time, were less frequent but not crowded as they are today. In Girgaon, virtually nobody had his own vehicle, not even a two-wheeler; many times, the young people, were overheard planning to take a scooter from a Parsee in the Prince's Street, whose job was to provide scooter on a rent at 5 rupees an hour, the plans, however, were never seemed to have come into the implementation. The taxis were available, but a *Girgaonkar* would prefer their way only in case of the exigencies like for going to the bus stand or railway station, with a full quorum of the family and half of the luggage in the house, in order to go to the native place, or for taking some family member to the hospital for immediate admission. The horse carts, popularly known as 'Victoria', were seen standing on various spots, the people used to engage a Victoria for going to or coming from areas as far as Parel and Colaba, they were primarily engaged for the convenience, when an excessive and ample luggage was to accompany the passengers, and not for a fancy as it is done nowadays. A Victoria would hold a large number of passengers and a sizeable luggage, but as its charges were somewhat higher than that of a taxi it was resorted to only when the situation demanded. The tramcars had been run in Mumbai by the BEST till the early 60s, where-after they were withdrawn from the street because their slow speed began hampering the progress of the other vehicles, which were speedier and therefore more suitable for a growing population of Mumbai. For the similar reasons, in the first 70's, the Victorias were forced to withdraw from the roads of Mumbai. In Girgaon, before the mid_60s, the sounds of clanking of the halting trams, humming of the starting trams, and clinking of the tram conductor's bells, coming through the silence of the night, could be heard by the *Girgaonkars*, till midnight approached, when they would be lying on the bed in a quiet home. Similarly, the sounds of creaking wheels, clucking of the coachman, hoofing horse, which were being heard in the silence of the night, vanished from Girgaon in the approach of the 8th decade, from when the Victorias were withdrawn from the roads of Mumbai.

THE TELEPHONE LINES IN GIRGAON

Having a phone line in the house was a rarest of the rare occurrence in Girgaon. The unfortunate house that a telephone line was provided, mostly at the behest of the employer who had wanted his particular employee to be assessable all the time, was set up with giving a compulsory social service of various types in the area. The members of home, that the phone was available, were required to, reluctantly, perform the role of calling any resident of the lane at any time of the day or night for attending to the phone calls addressed to him or her; speaking for more than a reasonable time on the phone, lingering on in the house in expectation of a call, enmity emanating from not being able to call a person when his call came, the offensive and ordering voice from the other end of the phone were the other problems that the phone owners were left to tackle.

THE STREET LIGHTS

Till the mid of the 60s, the streets, the lanes, and the by-lanes of Girgaon were lighted, in the night, by the street lights burnt at the gas. The shade of light emitting from those street lights was of a parrot green hue; the non-glaring, dim light so emitted from the street lamps would not pass beyond the 10 feet of the lamp post; in effect the atmosphere in the streets of silent night used to get mysterious and enigmatic. The lamp posts were made of cast-iron, designed after a Victorian style, and they were regularly painted, at a definite interval, in the silver colour; the lampshade of the street light would be of a thin glass, which was breakable even as a small stone striking it. Every evening, a person used to come running with an 18 foot stick in his hand, held by the help of his shoulder, and switch on the street lights by the help of clip attached at the top end of the stick, the switching on at one particular lamp post used to start 5 to 6 street lights in the row, he would then move to the next lamp post and then to the next, till the time all the lampposts in his allotted area were lighted; his time of arrival in the evening would change a little with the change of the season, he used to come by 7 in the summer and 5.30 in the winter. In the morning, all the street lights were switched off, before 7 o'clock, in a similar fashion.

THE PEDLARS

In the earlier time, the pedlars of different type, than that of today, were seen in Girgaon; a groundnut oil supplier and a salt vendor used to come to the doorsteps, the *kulfiwala*, who was spotted in all the seasons, would come in the nights of the summer up to third or fourth floor of the building, feigning a call from some home; seeing a *kulfiwala* at the doorstep would make it difficult for many people to avoid an impulse of having a cold *Kulfi* in the hot nights of the summer, in the way the *kulfiwala* would get quick business per floor. Besides the pedlars coming to the doorsteps, there were many who were visiting the lane; an ice cream seller used to come with a cylindrical vessel, wrapped with a red cloth, on a push cart and gave ice cream on a leaf for 5 *paise* and in a cone for ten *paise*, a *barf golawala* (a seller of the balls of grated ice sprinkled with the sweet syrup) would be thronged by the children for purchasing *gola* for self or for the elderly sisters at home, who would be peeping from the windows of the houses, similarly, the gas balloon vendor, coming with a gas cylinder on the push cart, would do a brisk business in the evening in every lane that he visited, he would be surrounded mostly by the parents of the children up to 5 years of age. For the purpose of the ladies, the seller of *gajras* and *venis* (small garland of the choicest fragrant flowers, meant to be worn in the hairdo) would go lane to lane calling only *vassvalle* (the fragrant), the ladies wishing to buy would call him as up as the fourth floor of the building.

A Muslim *pir* would visit a lane after lane by 10 o'clock in the night and attract the attention of the people by slightly playing a tiny drum with his right hand and solemnly reciting the *aytas* of the Koran', he would gather a coin or two, thrown from the above, by way of opening an umbrella, in his hand, in the direction of the road; in the early morning, a *Vasudev* used to come wearing his soiled white robe and a time worn head gear made of the peacock feathers, he would visit every lane playing the small bells in his hand and blabbing some rural, religious poems in non-perceivable words, he was never seen in the area after 8 (o'clock) in the morning. Sometimes, a 'jarimari' group used to visit the lane, the group would consist of a woman with a brass deity of the goddess on her head, a man beating a small drum, and a 'self-whipping man' with no clothes above the waist. Sometimes, the 'Dombaris' would suddenly come to the lane, before the noon or after 4 o'clock in the evening, and demonstrate the performance of their aerobic talent. A man would come with a 'Nandi Bail' (a pious ox), who would answer the questions of the children, such as about the results of the examination, by moving its head horizontally or vertically. Evidently, the intention of every visitor of such type was about earning some money, by way of alms, for filling the stomach.

THE POLICE, THE DADAS, AND THE MAWALIS

By and large a *Girgaonkar* was not required to face a law and order problem, even of a trivial nature. He was not required to see a police station in connection with any crime, even a small magnitude, because the course of his life would not offer any such circumstance that his visit to the police station was required. He had no reason to interact with anybody connected with the police department. Except, sometimes on the way, a *Girgaonkar* would pick up courage to refer his naughty little boy to a police *havaldar* and ask him, feigning a serious look, to scold a boy for his naughtiness, which a *havaldar* would do momentarily in his scary voice, but with a smile on his face; however, sometimes, a *havaldar* would take the jesting too far and make the father fall on his face by warning a child that, he should settle or he would put both, father and son, behind the bar.

However, there were some elements present in society, who would bring some excitement in otherwise quiet and peaceful movement of life in Girgaon. They were known as the *mawalis*, a group of wayward, school dropout boys and young men, existing in every lane. They could not just be called the *goondas* or miscreants, but they would be seen whiling their time away in and around the lane that they stayed by doing such acts, what an average *Girgaonkar* would be afraid even to think of doing. They would be, mostly, the unemployed youth, not because they could not get the jobs but because they did not have the temperament to serve meekly for years together, many of them were job drop outs more than being unemployed. They would take either no job or skip the existing job in order to live life without the hassles or tensions, which one had to face when in the job; moreover, by and large, they were the victims of the bad habits of consuming the country liquor or puffing the drugs, because of which the idea of getting stuck for the most part of the day, for some income, would not be an attractive proposition for them. Besides consuming country liquor and abusing drugs, they would pass the day playing cards with the stake, or in gambling of some or other type; sometimes, they would be playing the *Koyba* (a game played with three burly marbles of china clay) staking money. Though they did not have the job from which they could earn, they, however, were not deterred from earning money by way of running an illegal country liquor joint or a gambling den, or working on either of them, or giving a caring company to the whores, who were there in a few pockets of Girgaon. The *mawalis* in each lane would have their chief staying in the same lane, who was called the *Dada*; the *Dada* would be senior in age and would be experienced about the local crimes, he would have a lifestyle different from that of the *mawalis*, for he would be having substantial income from an illegal liquor joint or a gambling joint owned by him. He might have a murder or a few half murders to his credit, in relation of which he might have spent some months in jail; due to his criminal record, and illegal activities he would be in an interaction with the local police; because of his acquaintance with the policemen, mainly *havaldars*, they would spend some time in his company, when they had a reason to visit the lane in connection with any situation in and around the lane; his evident relationship and closeness with the police *havaldars* used to raise his respect in the eyes of his followers, meaning other *mawalis* of the lane, and the general residents of the lane. A 'Dada' would prove his reputation through his command over the *mawalis* of the lane; the *mawalis* would look to a 'Dada' for his advice and guidance, and his service in the matter of their nefarious activities, their release from the clutches of the police, when the need should arise, and intervention in matters of friction with other lanes.

The *Dada*, along with his gang of *mawalis* from the lane, would generate a strange idea, after a notion of patriotism, about the pride of the lane; he would harp on the pride of the lane and see to it that no disrespect was caused, to the same, by any action of anybody. The common residents of the lane, and especially the children of the lane, would get influenced by such an opinion about the pride of the lane, and they would tell boastfully, about the *Dada* and his gang from their lane, to their friends from another lane.

In the remaining time, which would remain after the pursuance of all the activities said earlier, the *mawalis* would, every now and then, take to the skirmishes, in the name of pride of the lane, with the gangs of other lanes for some trivial reasons; a skirmish would end up without any perceivable result, except breaking off of a few heads and throwing of a few soda water bottles, which, on more than one occasion, would harm nobody but create an unnecessary panic in the lane.

When the number of skirmishes with any lane would go too far then the condition for fighting would appear; fighting meant the gangs of two confronting lanes would have come to such a pass that the superiority of one of them after another had to be decisively established by means of the two gangs meeting head on, with a full strength, and fighting until one gang was subdued. The actual fighting would be preceded by casting of the challenges, accepting of the challenges, and responding to the challenges of each other. If the agreement were not struck in time, the date of the fight would be fixed by the challenging gang intimating the challenged gang as to on which day and at which time they would barge into their lane.

The conclusions of the fight would be different, and that would depend on the response shown by one of the parties in the fight. The supremacy of the challenging gang would be established if they barged at a given time and the challenged gang members preferred to offer no resistance by not coming face to face, or a challenged gang offered a fight at the first but soon vanished in the thin air, finding them incapable of sustaining the charge of the challenging gang. The supremacy of the challenged gang would be established if a challenging gang backed out of their challenge by not barging in the lane of a challenged gang at a pronounced time or if a challenging gang met with a stiff resistance from a challenged gang and took to heels from the defending lane.

Gone are the days when only the knives, iron rods, and hockey sticks were used in the fights, and when the fights used to take place forewarning the opposite sides, and giving a proper opportunity for preparing to fight back. It would appear nonsense in the age that the rivals are killed, stealthily and from a distance, by the revolvers.

CALLING FUNNY NAMES, A GIRGAONKAR BUSINESS

(The meanings of Marathi words are given at the end of chapter)

What is an appeal and what is ingenuity in calling a black person Blacky or calling Baldy to a person whose head is devoid of hair, and calling Shorty for one who has not reached 5 feet height. There are many ways of calling the person by chaffing names, of which some are tasteless, some are flavourless, and some are bogus and outrageous. If you want to get accustomed with various funny names or different tricks of jesting and chaffing, then you will have to walk about in the campus of that college that teaches that. Why going a zigzag way, I tell you right, you have to walk about in the lanes and by-lanes of Girgaon, keeping your eyes and ears open and bright.

A Girgaokar will call a bald individual *Airport*, a black woman *Avas*, that too in front of a gathering of the people. A name *Didfoot*, meaning Shorty, had emerged from Girgaon and now has become popular all over Maharashtra. If there is an opportunity to name a person, of course much subsequent to his naming ceremony at birth, for a local purpose than an imaginary power of a Girgaonkar will get reverberations just like any renowned writer gets when he discovers a new concept to pen it down.

A source of any such name is usually not detectable, but ingenuity in the names, so selected to ascribe to any person, appears evident. If, by chance, you happen to be a witness of such name discovery job you can return to know what that a think tank is meant and how it works.

It is a tale of the mid-60s, there used to sit a lot of wall painters in an open space, in front of a clinic of one doctor, whose practice was absolutely sluggish; the customers of the painters would also habitually end there, searching the painters, to remove a painter off for hiring the service of him. At the time when *Batata* Wada was available only in restaurants and not in every nook and corner of any street, that while one old painter from that group of the painters was jestingly named *Wada*. *Wada* is standing in the middle of the street and shouting vile words in one direction, the boys of the lane are laughing, showing the teeth, from the corners of the lane, the people have gathered on the balconies of their houses for watching a show on the road, was a typical sight which would meet the eyes on several occasions. After sometime older men of the lane used to drive the boys off and make *Wada* proceed. That programme of enraging *Wada* ran for quite a few years and stopped, only when Wada left the world. With *Wada,* there was one more old painter, who was named *Rawa*, but *Rawa* was unyielding in nature and did not show any angry reaction, and his attitude bored the name calling boys.

A girl from a respectable family was called *Chapati*, and she used to get enraged at calling her so. However, when once she caught a delinquent boy, red handed, by collar they stopped calling her by name on the road, although, while talking among themselves they would say, 'see, *Chapati* is coming', 'I heard *Chapati* is getting married soon' and so on. Another girl from another lane was called *Bhaji*, and she used to create a scene on the road as *Wada* would do, but once she ran on the road, with a sandal in hand, after a culprit boy, and the boys started getting scared with her and left going her way; *Bhaji*, it was heard, later married one of the boys calling her a name and continued with a happy life thereafter. One other girl was named *Chuna*, but, when she was called by that name by the boys, she would laugh shamelessly and get the boys feel demeaned.

The pedlars, going from street to street and lane to lane, would not be spared from keeping names and calling them with that to make them angry. In the nights of winter, a person with a flat container, held by his shoulder, containing *alepak*, used to come to sell his homemade product by going from an area to an area, he would call '*alpak, alepak*' repetitively to make people know about his arrival. Some naughty boys would respond stealthily to his yelling sound '*alepak, alepak* by '*Khaliwak, Khaliwak*' till the time he was in the area, he used to stand on his patience, but soon would become enraged, on many occasions. I remember once having seen him keeping the container on the nearby wall and running after the chaffing boys to get them.

In the morning time, in Girgaon, a *Vasudev* used to come wearing a soiled headgear, made of peacock feathers, and white clothes, which also would be soiled, he used to play small ball with his left hand and blabber religious, rural poems with non-perceivable words, in order to make the atmosphere of morning pleasurable, he would gather some coins given by some or other person for making earning for him. Once, in the mid-70s, I was going early morning to attend a sporting event of my college and I met my friend Prakash on the way, he also was going to Bombay Central place for attending to tuition classes. When we were walking together we came across *Vasudev*, he seemed to have become bewildered at the sight of Pakya coming from the distance. We passed Vasudev and walked a little further, however, no sooner did we pass *Vasudev* and go further than Pakya looked back in the direction of Vasudev and shouted, 'o, Vasudev, have you taken a bath ? *Vasudev* turned back, switched over from poetry to prose and the offensive words, instead of godly words, began flowing from his mouth. Mostly, that was a regular chore of Pakya.

The persons with any abnormality were also not left from keeping them names. An old man used to walk the area slowly with a trembling body, the boys had kept a name *Zukzuk for him*, and he was spotted murmuring abusive words, looking through his thick glasses, in a direction that his teasing name came. A boy, whose one leg had become thin like that of a peacock because of polio attack, used walk through the area as if he were dancing; the boys would call him *Thui-Thui*, that boy, however, used to answer that jesting with a smiling face of his. In one lane of Girgaon there stayed a building owner whose name was Nana (surname withheld), he used to stay in the same building that he owned, and perceptibly he did not have any other occupation than to wander about in the lane and into the building with the air of a building owner. Now this Nana had hydroxyl some years ago, and the people of the area soon christened him with a name *Andya* Nana; a name became acquainted with the people of the area, and so Nana also accepted that in spite of him. Once, one boy reached the home of Nana in order to deliver a message of somebody, he met the daughter in law of Nana at the door to whom he asked by habit whether *Andya* Nana was at home, she responded without an expression of any unusual manner and told him that the old man was in the upper room, Nana, also received a boy by shouting, 'which b . . . . d has come? Send him up'.

Not only the persons with deformity, but the persons who are victims of the tragic episode also would not be left from keeping names to them on the basis of the nature of tragedy, which they were subjected to. In the year 65-66, one boy from our lane attempted suicide on two consecutive and quick occasions, for he was disgusted with the unnecessary tough attitude of his financially incompetent father; fortunately, he, however, survived the attempts, but at the conclusion of his attempts the boys of the lane began calling him by the name of the pesticide that he had drunk for committing suicide. Might be because of the name kept for him and the chafing of the boys, but that boy did not attempt suicide anymore, and lived life happily thereafter.

The persons who were victims of an anomalous state of their existence were not only not left out but also were favourites with the Girgaonkars for finding out the names and tricks to tease them. In one lane of Girgaon, there stayed one middle aged person, his name was Savalya and his character was absolutely effeminate. The boys of the lane that Savalya stayed would find out different tricks to tease and harass him; Savalya was staying with the brother's family, in the brother's own room, which was on the ground floor of the building, and whose doors would open onto the lane. The boys of the lane, when they would have a pang, would drag to the lane a large gate garland, which would have been thrown outside a Parsee hall by 11 o clock in the night, after a wedding party having had done; a garland as such dragged near the lane would be fixed, in the midnight, to the closed door of the room that Savalya stayed, and a notification about a Savalya's wedding would be written with chalk on the closed door; it was decided that the lanes people would wake up the next morning hearing the high pitched foul language of Savalya. Once the boys, at the night time, removed a just then stuck bill of a Marathi movie 'ha khel savalyacha' (this is a show of savalya) and stuck that, on the door of the room that Savalya stayed, it goes without saying that the rapid rounds of dirty words were again shot in the early hours of the next morning.

The domain of terror in Girgaon was reigned by the Dadas and the mawalis, but those people also were not left out of the clutches of the Girgaonkars for assigning them names like *Badkya* Dada, *Chapat* Dada, *Kalya* Waman, *Batlya* Suresh, and so on.

Sometimes, a name ascribed to a particular person would go on to his next generation also. In the years 65-66, a new family came for residing in the area, the boys of the family were OK looking, but the father was totally a squint, what's to say that the boys of the area started teasing those boys of a new family by calling them *Kanya*. A concubine staying in the area had the two/three boys born out of her last keepers; a father, of one of the children of her, who was her last keeper, and who had been a wealthy man once and now became an old man with a measly income, would be coming to the area, under the pretext of caring for a child but keeping an eye on his once while concubine, and called his son by shouting his name from the street; the boys of the area slyly found out the name of an old man and began calling that boy of him with the name Lalji, which obviously was a name of that old man. The name became so popular that a half brother of the boy also would call him, sometime, with that name. In one building near Alankar Talkies, the Gujaratis and the Marathis were, amicably, cohabiting, and spoke the language of each other among themselves. In the late 70s, one old person in the building was ascribed the name *Teku*, ostensibly, because of his habit of standing unnoticed behind anybody. That old man died after some years, and afterwards that name was given, by virtue of hereditary rights, to his son; that son of an old man also died after some more years, and now his son, who is a 40 year old man, even today has to face a question, 'kem *Teku*, kem chho?' (yes *Teku*, how are you ?)

Some names were passed from generation to generation, whereas some names were limited to the lifetime of a person, then some other names existed only for a temporary period. A man, who was caught by the police during the riot in 68, was called *Kelapav* for some time after his release, whereas one person was called *Havaldar* only when he wore a particular dress; a person was named and called *Gavathi* Rajesh till the time he abandoned his recently adopted 'Rajesh Khanna hairstyle' and reverted to his first one.

Geographically speaking some names were confined to a building, and some to a lane or a street, but some other broke all confines and became popular in the wider area. I remember having seen a show created by *Wada* in the bustle at Thakurdwar junction and as well at Prarthana Samaj crossing.

Mostly the chosen names were a person based, but in some cases they were a profession based, horse cart men were mostly teased with calling them *Gajkaran*, whereas the bus driver and the bus conductors were called diesel *Chor* and *Bablya* respectively; when called names by anybody from the road these people would be bewildered, but could do nothing leaving the tasks at hand, it was also different that the passengers in the vehicle could not control laughing. A horse cart man sometime would wave his whip in the air, but an object used to be beyond the range of his long whip. In the same fashion, when travelling by train, a Railway Food Stall was yelled at *Basi Wada*, and the gangmans working on the tracks were called *Kamchor*; here the situation used to be different that a teasing person would be in motion.

It was not heard anybody having left Girgaon because he was teased or called names, but it was evident that a name would not leave a person even though he had left Girgaon. Once I met my old school friend on Vile Parle Railway Station, and we continued talking, standing on the railway platform itself; suddenly a cry *Bokya* came from the running train, on the track yonder, going toward Church Gate Station, and my friend waved his hand in the direction of the passing train, on asking him about his unexpected reaction to a call from the train he said that, before he had been staying in one of the wadis of Girgaon, where he was named and called *Bokya*, also he said that, he had left Girgaon many years since, but he still would get such calls from a bus or a train, in any part of Mumbai, to which he habitually would respond. One girl cum woman from Girgaon was named *Pakodi*, at length, she married to a boy from a village in the western suburb and went there to stay; nobody knew how, but her that name followed her to that village within 2/3 months of her coming there; as it was, the village was infamous for mischievousness and everybody began calling her by that name from every nook and cranny and in the every small street of the village. When complained, her husband would laugh off the situation and show no inclination to defy the people of the village that he had stayed many years since. Her brother took some miscreants from Girgaon to scare the villagers, but they did not relent. Now that woman is quite old, but nobody in the village knows her real name as yet.

As ragging is considered ideal for the freshers to tune up with the mischievous atmosphere of the college, the ways of jesting in Girgaon are felt necessary for coping with that nature of life in Girgaon. The Girgaonkars joke and banter for helping each other, when anyone begins floating in the air at a touch of small success, to keep the feet on the earth. A boy from the area accomplished decent education and got a decent job, by the grace of god he earned his promotion soon and he began hurrying up now and then on a motorbike, dressed immaculately and wearing a necktie and so; he started avoiding his once friends from the area. The boys soon named the boy *Zatliman* and started calling him by that name, every now and then, wherever he might be seen. Soon *Zatliman* came to his senses and began mingling with his friends as before. Similarly, if anybody briefly earned some considerable amount of money and began showing off his moneyed situation in the area then he just was harassed by calling him 'this *Sheth*' and 'that *Sheth*'.

Some names had been mild just like *Dhapnya*, *Tagya*, *Batarya*, *Varvantya*, *Nakadya*, whereas some were terrible like *Andya* Nana. The names like *Popat*, Taxi, and so, chosen after the colour of school uniform, were falling in the listless category.

Many times, that aspect of jesting used to go too far and a dispute or a fight was taking place; many persons were living tremendously and were afraid to tackle any new venture, and the initiative was marred. But, if you have to stay in Girgaon a name or jesting would come your way anytime, and you ought to possess the ability to sustain that onslaught.

Isn't it right ?

See how my friend *Vangya*, sitting beside, is smiling tongue in cheek.

MEANINGS OF THE MARATHI WORDS IN THIS CHAPTER

Alepak :—a small cake of the mixture of crushed ginger and sugar

Andya :—a funny version of word anda (an egg)

Avas :—a no moon night

Bablya :—a rural boy

Badkya :—a funny version of word badak (a duck)

Basi :—stale

Batata Wada :—a deep fried small ball of boiled potatoes coated with thin dough of gram flour

Batarya :—a frog eyed boy

Batlya :—shorty

Bhaji :—deep fried small balls of dough of gram flour mixed with any vegetable

Bokya :—a funny name for male cat

Chapat :—a flat faced man

Chapati :—thinly flattened dough of wheat flour, baked on griddle

Chor :—a thief

Chuna :—lime

Dhapanya :—a funny looking bespectacled person

Didfoot :—one and half foot

Gajkaran :—ringworm

Gavathi :—boorish

Havaldar :—a police constable

Kalya :—blacky

Kamchor :-a work shirker

Kanya :—a squint eyed person

Kelapav :—banana bread

Khaliwak :—bend down

Nakadya :—a funny looking nosy person

Pakodi :—deep fried small balls of dough of gram flour

Popat :—parrot

Rawa :—coarsely ground wheat

Tagya :—stubby boy

Teku :—a support

Thui Thui :—a dancing of peacock

Sheth :—wealthy man

Vangya :—a funny version of word vanga (Brinjal)

Varvantya :—a funny version of word varavanta (stone grinder)

Zatliman :—a funny version of word Gentleman

Zukzuk :—a funny sound of running steam engine of the railway

PART - 2

THE PORTRAITS

SHAMU PAWANKAR

It was not long ago since the great movement for the integrated Maharashtra, popularly known as '*Sanyukta* Maharashtra *Chalwal*', was over; the state of Maharashtra was cast, along with Mumbai as its capital, as per the populous demand, though not without the martyrdom of many lives. The life in the city of Mumbai, before long, crawled back to the normal and continued as smoothly as it had been before the movement. As an aftermath of the movement, the communists, who had been holding firm to their citadels in the working class areas many years since, tried to extend their tentacles in the middle class areas like Dadar and Girgaon, their efforts, however, did not seem to have been meeting with a perceivable success. Some local leaders, with an endemic communistic inclination, however, were elected as the corporators to the municipal corporation from some wards of the middle class areas; as the communists could gain some power, at the local level, in the middle class area there cropped up the latest communist party workers, who, in fact, were not particularly much acquainted with the party line, principles, beliefs, and policies; such party workers had no other perceivable job to do except to move sheepishly along their mentors, who would be visiting the wards of them as a routine, or attending any public programmes in the area. The leaders had no option available to them except to carry on with the available lot of the workers till the time either they were metamorphosed into the perfect party workers, or a new batch of the dedicated workers was mobilised. On many occasions, the local residents of the area would be after such workers either to gather information or to get done the work, which, more often than not, would be of a typical local nature; in turn, such party workers began gathering a significant importance, among the locals, which, at a time, was like a non bearable burden to them; they used to go about with an air of authority and power, which, in fact, was several miles away from them; the suddenness, in which they had been catapulted into the position, had made them uneasy in their behaviour, actions, and body language. The days were of the first few years of the 60's.

Shamu Pawankar was one of the communist workers of that description, and his area of operation was from Gai*wadi* to Prarthana Samaj, in Girgaon; in those days, Shamu was prominently seen, with or without the company of the local corporator, in and around any gathering of public interest.

Shamu had a decent height, a lean and agile body, and a remarkable posture; at that time he was about 30 years of age. He was always to be found neatly dressed, with a full sleeve shirt nicely tucked in the medium bottomed pants, and with nothing but the *chappals* as footwear. He used to back-comb his thick hair tightly, which used to produce significant impact to his clean shaven face, whose striking features were a bluntly pointed chin and a noticeably pointed nose. His movements were brisk, and he habitually used to wear a casual, inviting smile on his face; in the result, he was more or less a likable person in the area, and people used to feel comfortable with being around him.

Chewing betel leaf *paan* consistently was the prominent feature of Shamu, whenever he was seen he was to be found with his mouth making the constant movements out of chewing of *paan*, and lips and tongue coloured reddened by the juice of *paan*. Shamu's habit of chewing a *paan*, however, would come to his release on many occasions; if someone stopped Shamu on his way and asked him in connection with the progress of some work, which he was supposed to answer because of a position in which he had fitted himself, then Shamu would prevent the inquirer in a miming style, with his palm raised in the air before the inquirer's face, and look around for a convenient corner; on finding such corner at any distance in the surrounding, Shamu would reach there, without any haste, and spit voluminously in order to make his mouth speech-worthy. This process would take quite a substantial period of time, and the inquirer would lose some aggressiveness with which he had confronted the fugitive, also the inquirer would be confused by the counter questions put by Shamu; in the meantime, Shamu would have been called, from the opposite side of the road, by a member of the similar inquisitive specie, Shamu would dash quickly to the other bank of the road, in a fashion of a crow flying from a tree to tree, keeping an eye on an earlier inquirer, whom he had dodged, lest he followed, joined with the new one, and reinstated an inquiry with a renewed zest.

Shamu also had a habit of consuming country liquor, but that habit of his was not apparent to the public eye. Nobody from the general public had ever claimed to have actually seen him drinking any offensive drink, but the reddish eyes and dopey face with which he would meet on any particular morning would mention clearly of his programme of the previous night. That habit of Shamu, however, had not gone too far to become a cause of concern for his public image in the locality.

The children would look up to the Shamu's face, if they happened to find themselves in the crowd around him, with a respectful fear, because they had, in their mind, a fearsome image of the communists, which might have been created through what that they were overhearing their elders discussed among themselves, about the communists, from time to time; the children were wondered to observe how the people about Shamu's age would deal fearlessly, conveniently, and, sometimes, even contemptuously with him.

Nobody had an idea as to how Shamu earned his livelihood. The elders had an inkling that Shamu owned a printing press, but that idea had emanated out of the manner with which Shamu was moving around in the area; I, however, chanced to discover what that Shamu exactly was doing; one of the school friends of mine was staying in the lane that Shamu was staying, my friend told me that Shamu was working as a canvasser for the printing presses, and earning the commission for the jobs that he would prefer to the presses; it seemed, he was dabbling in the political sphere only because he had been required to do so by his profession, which has a strong and un—severing connection with the political activities, for the politics cannot be run without the use of printed materials like handbills, banners, posters, and leaflets. Shamu was not from a well to do or even a middle class family; he was discovered to have been staying, with his family, in a dingy room after the fashion of Girgaon. Shamu had a mediocre background, an insufficient education, and a measly income, but his earnestness of working for the people was genuine, nobody could doubt about the realness of his innate tendency of serving the people.

The euphoria of the movement had died off long ago, and the communistic mentor of Shamu lost the next corporation election. Shamu was left with no party or principles or activities, he found himself in an extremely difficult situation like that of a child lost in a fair. Shamu held to the ground bravely for quite a some time. Many times, in the ensuing years thereafter, he was seen in a melee outside the office of a congress candidate for the election, but he was seen being paid no attention by the workers or leaders of his once rival party. Shamu hobnobbed with the congress party for quite a large number of years and with a considerable obstinacy, and eventually he managed to get some success in creating a ground for him in that party; but the ground level to which he was kept for later many years, without any perceivable hopes for an exaltation, was not a sustainable situation for him in the light of his advancing age; it was embarrassing for him to have been associated with the ground level workers, that mostly comprised the young workers with a youth-worthy vigour; it was quite a difficult situation to cope with for him. During that period, many times, frustration overtook Shamu, but he had no means available to him to vent it out, but some fair period was lurking in the near future for Shamu.

The eighth decade began and by that time Indira Gandhi had created a stir in the country by her radical economic measures and her strong and successful handling of an international problem of Bangladesh; Indira Gandhi and her congress earned an enormous following in the country. In that situation, Shamu had no other alternative but to hold on to the congress party and remain contented with any position in which he was kept. At that time, Shamu was seen moving around with the local youth leaders and the Congress party workers, who had been holding a perceivable power and influence at the time, but their way of looking down at Shamu would emphasize his subdued role in the party; Shamu, however, had no choice but to keep on moving, with his aging face, in the company of young workers.

Some bright time, however, emerged for Shamu. The emergency was declared in the 1975, and all the congress workers received a non pronounced coverage of prerogatives, security, and dignity, in addition to the self-assumed authority, supported by the stringent rules of the emergency. The days of emergency passed happily for the workers like Shamu and also for some peace loving people of the country; the opposition, however, was not missing an opportunity provided to them for whipping up public sentiment. The men of industries, who were commonly known as the capitalist then, were already unhappy with the socialistic inclination of the government, which had created a considerable amount of obstructions for the smooth sailing of the industries. The media were made ready, as they are always made in a situation like so, to criticize the government on account of its policies and excesses. The international press was done, as it is ever in the case of India, to admonish and defame the Indian government, in an international scenario, by highlighting its shortcomings.

The period of emergency passed with many disputatious events, which caused mixed reflections of the people; the general discipline was welcome, however, some excesses in the case of the media censorship, the family planning programme, and the 'high handed' attitude of the men in the authority triggered anti-government feelings, mostly the younger generation was targeted, for invoking provocation, by the opposition parties. At length, the emergency was withdrawn after 19 months of its imposition; the government yielded to the pressure of the opposition parties and declared fresh elections. The new euphoria emerged in the country that was the euphoria of the Janata Party, which was created out of a conglomeration of various parties with a different ideology of each of them. Shamu felt the vibrations in the grass root level well in time, for he belonged to the grass root level, and he was familiar with the knack of feeling the vibrations in time; Shamu had become a veteran political activist after having spent a significant amount of time in the hubbub of political happenings. Shamu joined the Janata Party and worked for it in the elections, which were declared immediately after the emergency was withdrawn; when the Janata Party won the elections, Shamu duly partook in the rejoicing, along with a new bunch of compatriots, after a fashion of a revolutionary rejoicing in a long awaited success of the revolution. The period of two years, of the Janata Party government, passed away lack-lustrously, the people had slowly understood that the revolution that was much boasted about was confined to only presenting of the sweet dreams, which were, in fact, far away from the realization; the people got disillusioned. The Janata Party got disintegrated, and Indira Gandhi won the next election. Shamu, however, was not as disheartened as the general public was, for he was a seasoned political worker, who had seen many risings and downfalls. The changed circumstances did not affect the life of Shamu to any great extent, except that he had to face a phase of inactivity for some time, but he did not leave tramping on his long trodden way as one does not leave breathing when alive. Shamu did not try to set a foot back in Congress; to rejoin the Congress, after having worked against them in their difficult years, was not as easy for Shamu as it was for the shameless prominent leaders; for a worker of Shamu's stature, it was more difficult than easy to go back to the congress without meeting with the offensive remarks and a humiliating treatment, which his age would not have allowed him to bear with. Shamu continued to live in a limbo for some time.

It was beginning of the 80's, and by that time Shivsena, a regional party, was more than a decade old and had established a formidable hold on the populace of Mumbai; Shivsena was doing a significant work in the lower layer of the society and also in the municipal corporation, which it had managed to capture by dint of its network in the middle and lower class areas of Mumbai; during that period, Shivsena, with the help of a muscle power in its background, was literally holding the reins of the city in its hands. That time, it was whispered that Shivsena was facilitated to be established and flourished, in an attempt to weaken the dreaded grip of the Communists over the city, by the congress itself. The rumours were never proved to be true, but, however, in the beginning years of Shivsena, there had been many street fights between the groups of the workers of the communist party and Shivsena. The communists were already known for delivering the miserable feelings, by which the mill owners and industrialists—the main purveyors of the much needed party fund—were haunted. The youths easily got attracted to the new organization, as till then no platform was available to them, and now that was provided to them, at the very threshold of their homes, in the form of Shivsena *Shakhas*, which were continually bustled with the presence and activities of the workers; as for the activities for youths, they were amply made available on a day to day basis, in contrast to the earlier era in which the political parties would gear up the organizational activities only when an outstanding issue cropped up.

Shamu, a one-time communist, entered in that wonderland, which had been around and conjuring him; Shamu slowly got himself penetrated, as a worker, in Shivsena and began getting involved in the social-political activities organised, in the area, under the auspices of a local Shivsena leader, whom Shamu had submitted his devotion to. But there, in his new party, Shamu was not expected to receive any more power than what was given to a simple worker.

A half cooked Communist, a Congress hobnobber, a Janata Party guest, and finally an average Shivsena worker—a strange course of Shamu's political life had made his character a bunch of confusing traits; but the experience that was thrust on him by the time was not to go into the waste, in any case.

Shamu involved himself in the 'Ganapati *Mandal*' of the lane that he resided, and, soon, he could create a prominent role for him in the '*Mandal*'. Over a period of several years, the size of 'Ganapati Idol' grew year by year, and so grew the coffer of the '*Mandal*', and, evidently, the actual financial situation of Shamu did not lag behind. Thereafter, it was heard, Shamu was conducting some small time but useful schemes for the senior citizens and poor school going children of the lane; over a period of time, many older people and children had been recipients of the benefits of the Shamu's schemes.

I left Girgaon in the first 90's. I am not in a habit of keeping track of the persons, who do not occur to my mind unless they are about. For many years, I had not had any knowledge of Shamu. Recently, I had a casual conversation with my relative in Girgaon; in the conversation there was some reference of the lane in which Shamu was staying. I, without any purpose, absently inquired about Shamu with my relative.

'Shamu is dead, a few years ago,' he told me, nonchalantly.

BABICHA NAVRA

'Babicha Navra', meaning the Babi's husband, was the name by which we knew or called our childhood tailor. I did not know why he was called by the name Babicha Navra instead of Ramchandra Kaka, Sakharam Kaka or such other names. In fact, I do not remember having seen Babi anytime in my childhood, or even later, as much I had a chance to see or deal with Babicha Navra. I even remember having shouted, 'Babicha Navra had come', in front of him, when he had come to our home in one of the Ganapati days, to which he had responded with his typical sheepish smile, without an iota of resentment on his face. Even on one or two occasions, I remember, he had given me a message to reach my father that he had mentioned about him as Babicha Navra, like, 'tell your father that Babicha Navra has completed a coat', or, 'tell your father that Babicha Navra has obtained the lining cloth'.

After purchasing the fabric materials on any Sunday, much prior to the beginning of Ganapati festival, we were taken by our father to the shop of Babicha Navra, which was at the beginning of Mugbhat X Lane; as soon as we should come near the shop we could see Babicha Navra, who used to be always found wearing a striped *lenga* and a full sleeve shirt, with the upper three buttons open and the sleeves shabbily folded up to the elbow; that was his usual clothes, when he was to be found in the shop and anywhere in the nearby area; only once he was seen in white pants reaching up to his chest, and a white shirt tucked into the pants, when he had come to our home on one of the Ganapati days. He was a short man with a little pot belly and his hair, which was curled and unkempt, had started receding from the forehead; his eyes were protruding like a frog and they always would appear bloodshot; no-one knew why his eyes always should appear red coloured, but one easily could conjecture that they were so due to either a sleeping disorder or a drinking habit of his. His face would betray the expressions of an idiotic schoolboy, and his age seemed the same, what it would have been ten years before and what it would be ten years after. On seeing us, he would welcome my father with his typical inwardly sheepish smile, and no sooner did we enter the shop than he would send any person at hand to fetch some glasses of tea, for, it appeared, he used to think that the only way of expressing the pleasure on arrival of anybody of any significance was serving him with the tea, as soon as possible; the servant sent for bringing the glasses of tea would, purposely or not, bring odd number of glasses, and in an ensuing confusion, the situation would arise that even a small child had to drink the tea, at the odd hours of the late evening, holding a glass of tea in hand, on the street, in front of the shop. That tea party only used to occur when my father would come to his shop, along with the children, for giving the cloths for making the dresses; in our subsequent, numerous, follow up visits to his shop, without a father with us, we would meet only a sullen face of his.

In our home, the main occasion, to make the new clothes, was the Ganapati festival. On one Sunday, much prior to the festival, my father would take us to the cloth shop in Girgaon and purchase the fabric material for each one of the children, the choice of the children would be considered, to some extent, only for the shirt cloth material, but for the pants the only criteria would be a dull colour of the textile, so the clothes should remain unstained for the long time. After purchasing the fabric, we would proceed to the shop of Babicha Navra; after a tea party as detailed earlier, he would take the measurement of each of the children, but before doing that he would go through his soiled notebook for referring to the measurements taken on the previous occasion; he, however, would leave the attempt in no time. He would take the measurement afresh and write the figures, in pencil, on one of the light-coloured cloth pieces of ours, mentioning that afterward he would transfer the measurement figures to the notebook and rub out the figures on the cloth; in the result of that, when the clothes were ultimately received, we would find that one of the shirts of an unfortunate brother was marked with all the pencil figures on the collar, or the back, or the hand of it; the pre washing of the clothes, before the function began, was not available, because the clothes would have been delivered at the last moment before the function.

The fabric materials were given to Babicha Navra for making the dresses at least three weeks before the Ganapati festival would begin; at the time of undertaking the job he used to produce a commitment to make the clothes finished in one week. We used to have our first shock when we would go to his shop, after 8 or 10 days of giving the cloth to him, for bringing the clothes; we would encounter him with a question mark on his face as to what was it that brought these children to his shop, we would open the subject about the clothes and his face would flash as if he remembered something that he had forgotten, then he would begin asking questions about the number and colours of the cloth pieces; when we should answer his questions to his satisfaction he would take out the bundles of cloth pieces, tied by the strings made out of the wasted cloth, from the down portion of the cupboard and from the upper shelf; the next job, which we had to do, was to find out the bundle of our cloth pieces, from the numerous bundles of cloth pieces of the seemingly harried customers of his. After identifying our cloth material, Babicha Navara would ask us to come after four days for collecting the dresses; after four days, and then after two days, and again after four days, in an anxiety of seeing our new dresses our visits to his shop would be several; our hopes would be rekindled by a new promise given by him on each visit; at length, the Ganapati day would arrive, but our trouble of visiting his shop would not leave us, however, in our every visit to his shop we would be happy bit by bit, each time, by seeing our clothes in the different developing stages like a collarless shirt, a button less or buttonholes-less pants and so on.

We were supposed to wear the new dresses in the get-together held in the evening of the second last day of the Ganapati festival, we would not have received the clothes till morning of that day, on that day of the get-together we would begin visiting the shop of Babicha Navara right from 9 o'clock in the morning, he eventually would give the clothes by 5 o'clock in the evening; after bringing the clothes home, we would wear them in a hurry for the trial purpose, and soon we would begin finding that, in one shirt, one button was missing whereas, in one pants, the buttons were alright but the buttonholes were missing, in yet another pants or shirt the buttonholes and the buttons were not matching to each other; some dresses would bear the mill marks at the prominent places whereas the other dresses would bear the tailor marks at the difficult places. We used to wear the clothes as they were received, for celebrating the evening, and from the next day we would begin visiting the shop of Babicha Navra, for another 15 days, to get the dresses repaired.

The business of Babicha Navra did not seem to have been brisk; the numerous bundles of fabric pieces in his shop were the indication of his mismanagement of the business and not of his steep business; his labour management was seemingly poor, for every time we would find a new face, in his shop, in his assistant.

Babicha Navra remained to be our family tailor till the end of the 60s, by then the grown up brothers began going to the other more organised tailoring shops in Girgaon, as by that time quite a few such shops had come up in Girgaon; the tailors of these shops would take the measurements systematically, take the trial before finalising the clothes, use the quality material for stitching the clothes, and give the delivery of the clothes, more or less, on time. Slowly we forgot to go to Babicha Navra for our tailoring jobs.

At that time, meaning the last years of the 60s, we learnt from some source that Babicha Navra had kept one woman as a concubine; it was a subject of mockery among the persons who knew Babicha Navra, it was a matter of curiosity for everyone as to what that woman ought to have seen in Babicha Navra and his means to accept him as her keeper.

Babicha Navra and his shop was seen, at the turn of the Mugbhat X Lane, till the mid of the 70s, but afterwards it came to our ears that he had sold the shop and also his room and shifted to his native place, where he had been living with Babi, her children, his concubine, and her children, in the same house.

Even today when I go to Girgaon and happen to pass by the Mugbhat X Lane and look at the place, where the shop of Babicha Navra was, the memories of my childhood errands there, in pursuance of the clothes, send a shiver down my spine.

APPA TADGE

Appa Tadge was a fearsome person in the lane that we were staying in Girgaon. Appa could not just be called a criminal or miscreant or gangster, but he, undoubtedly, was a man, who used to encourage and support the nefarious and troublesome activities in the lane, by which the peace in the lane was disturbed on more than one occasion; for the pursuance of such activities, Appa had in his hand a group of criminally inclined, wayward, and precocious young boys, to whom he used to play a godfather. In other lanes, by the custom of that time, there were gangs of wayward boys from that particular lane, the chief of which was known as *Dada* of that lane. A *Dada* would come up from a rank and file, and he might have a few murders and half murders, in the past, to his credit; *Dada* might take actual part in the fights, whenever they took place, or made available his acumen in directing and guiding the boys, who would take an active part in the fights that *Dada* was not to participate. But Appa was not a *Dada*, for he did not meet the parameters of eligible *Dada*. The boys of Appa's gang were also not as daring as the boys of some dreaded gangs of other lanes were. Moreover, Appa's boys were somewhat interested in satiating their unhealthy, bad habits than getting their heads broke in the fights.

Appa was not picking fights with his equals, or persons of stronger capacities. His way of spreading terror was tepid, he would chase the beggars out of the lane with a stick in hand, or hit a madman strayed in the lane; sometimes, he would pick a fight with a simple passer-by, under some or other pretext, and acquaint him with a fear in the mind of a mouse trapped in the captivity of a ferocious cat. Once, Appa had so much beaten a madman, who had taken a shelter in the lane, with a stick that the madman died after some hours. Appa, in an inebriated state, would dash in the direction of a couple, consisting of husband and wife, passing by the lane and give them a sense of fearful dizziness, a couple would speed up in a frenzied state of mind and pass the lane as quickly as possible, looking back every now and then until they were out of the proximity of Appa and they reached the main road.

In the beginning of the 60's, Appa was in his late 30's. He had a large stomach, medium height, and heavy body. His half grey hair on his head was curly and short and had a tendency to grow upward than in any other direction; his bloodshot eyes would elevate his ferocious appearance and his slightly protruding teeth were always evident from his rugged face; from a distance, Appa would appear as if he were snarling at anybody, when, in fact, he would simply be talking to that person.

When at home, Appa was always seen in a homely attire, which consisted a half khaki pants, reaching up to the knees, and a half sleeve banyans, of a white turned to a yellowish colour; his notion of the extent of his home, however, was inclusive of his home, his shop, a whole lane before it, and the nearby by-lanes; anywhere in the whole of that area, Appa was to be found only in his homely dress, at any time of the day and night. His enormous stomach was not able to keep his half pants at the place where it should be, and it was always found tied on a waist portion under his stomach. Appa did not believe in an extravaganza of the clothes like the shirts and the full pants, which he was resorting to only when he had a reason to go to the region, much beyond the region of his 'home'. Sometimes, when on such an errand, he was also seen going away from the lane wearing a *sadra* and a *lenga*, the colour of which would be whiter than that of his banyan.

Till the beginning of the 60's, Appa owned two rooms, side by side, opening onto the main road of the lane. One room was used for the staying purpose by the family of Appa and in the other room Appa had his fabrication workshop. How much Appa was earning from the fabrication jobs and whether that income was sufficient for his family was a matter of curiosity for everybody, for his family to support was reasonably large, consisting of his wife, a son and many daughters, and his fabrication business appeared, more or less, to be listless. However, Appa's financial condition did not appear to be that miserable as he was often noticed taking his family on periodic trips to his native place, which was a village beyond Pune. Whatever might be his income from his workshop, but his workshop was certainly a reliable source of the instruments of fighting, in case of need, for the miscreants of the lane.

In the 60's, the cricket test matches used to take place in India only once in two years, mainly in the winter seasons, unlike in these days when the cricket matches, whether tests or any of their newer forms, are played almost every month of the year. Also, unlike in this age, in the 60's the only source of the 'ball to ball' details of the match was the running commentary broadcast on the radio. The radio sets, however, were not to be found in that number that even the T.V. sets are found in the present days; very few well to do houses would have the radio sets, the control of which was never left to anybody else than the head of the family or his arrogant, upstart son; therefore, the task of fulfilling a desire of listening to the running commentary of the cricket match, in a cosy and comfortable environment, was not easy to accomplish; for that, either you had to have a friend of your age, whose family possessed a radio set and who was a duffer in studies compared to you and you had proved to be helpful to him in solving the problems of mathematics or geometry, or you had to prove yourself able to a lady of the house, which had a radio set in it, by occasionally going to the market to bring some items for her as per her instructions. At that time, that luxury would be made available by Appa to everybody, who wished to avail that. Appa had in his shop one radio set, which had been always placed on the inside of his shop; on any other days than that of test cricket matches, 'Radio Ceylon' and 'Vividh Bharti' played on that radio set would not be audible out of the shop, unless one strained his hearing capacity. When the test matches would begin in India, and especially in Mumbai, Appa used to place his radio set prominently in front of the shop, facing the road. A small crowd of the boys and men of the lane, joined occasionally by the flitting passers-by, would gather in front of the shop of Appa, in order to listen to the commentary, and intermittently offer their own comments on the game with an enthusiasm, which at a time would be greater than that with which game proceeded. The many sounds of roars, clapping, and laughter, being spontaneous reactions to the sensational and amusing happenings on the cricket ground, would be emanating from the group gathered in front of the shop of Appa; such spasmodic, exultant uproars would be heard throughout the lane, till the time match got over for the day. I remember having seen the radio set of Appa being garlanded on some occasions, when a century or five wicket haul was reached by an Indian batsman or bowler. The days, when the cricket matches were played, would the wintry days, and the chilly atmosphere would be prevailing with severity, because, at that time, the population of Mumbai was not as thick as it is today, so as to emit a sufficient heat in the alleviation of the severe chilliness in the atmosphere. In those wintry days, listening to the radio commentary, standing in front of Appa's shop, in warm sunshine had been quite a pleasurable experience; those who had an opportunity to enjoy those joyful moments would not forget them at any stage of life, and with that, Appa and his radio set would undoubtedly stay in their memory till they live.

In the wintry days, the events of two types were taking place, in our lane, under the auspices of Appa. One was the *Kabaddi* (then known as *hututu*) matches arranged with teams of other lanes in the vicinity, and another was a cycling record; the former was a team sport whereas the latter was an individual performance in the name of the lane. In case of the *Kabaddi* match, on the day of the match the preparation used to begin from 7 o'clock in the evening. A powerful bulb would be hung, in the middle of the lane, by a strong rope tied between the railings of the first floors of two opposite buildings; the wire from the bulb would be reaching Appa's shop for the supply of electricity. Some enthusiastic boys of the lane would undertake to sweep the desired area, which would soon be as clean as a looking glass. The lines would be drawn, with the help of a brush and lime water, as per the rules of the game. One or two harbingers of the visiting team would arrive by 8 o'clock, ostensibly, to review the arrangement, but they would pass their time talking sweet nothing with the leading hosts, with Appa overlooking them. At length, the whole of the guest team would gather and prepare for a start of the match. The bulb would have been lighted, in the meantime, illuminating the required area, over powering the soft, greenish light of the street gas lamps. The residents would enjoy watching the game, which was not to proceed beyond 10.30, from their galleries and balconies, with pleasant chilliness of December or January enveloping their bodies. The match would have been over, and the lane, after a dying murmur of some time, was engulfed by a silence; with a large bulb having switched off long ago, the green, dim light of the street gas lamps would have again pervaded the lane.

In the month of December or January, the information and details about the cycling records in the other lanes would appear percolating into our lane; the topic would be the foremost in the discussion among the boys and the men of our lane, when they gathered in the corner of the lane or in the galleries of their buildings. Appa would be fully apprised of such challenging events in the other lanes, he then would make him resolve to organize a similar event in the lane, for our lane should not be seemed to be lagging behind in any such activities. A day would be fixed, and the event publicised by way of writing by a chalk on the blackboard, hung prominently at the corner of the lane.

Rashi, who would be an obvious choice of Appa for such an event that incessant cycling ability was required, would be moving in and around the lane with an air of importance. Rashi Bandivadekar was a chosen disciple of Appa. He, at that time of the early 60's, was a young man of 25 years of age. He was a lean and thin man of an average height, and he used to sport a prominent moustache on his thin lips; a lock of thick, soft hair on his head would be lingering always on his forehead. He was a supple bodied person, and he used to walk, bowing forward, in a quivering way. The boys would look up to Rashi in some astonishment and discuss some tales, true or fictitious, about him; one, which I remember, is that once Rashi had found himself in the clutches of the members of a rival gang, in some distant area, at which time he managed to escape and come cycling to our lane, as fast as only an Olympian could do.

Finally, a beginning day of the event would appear; Rashi would be ready, attired in a white dress, betraying anxiousness on his face. By 9 o'clock in the morning, the event would be flagged off by none other than Appa, beforehand breaking a coconut on the stone and sprinkling coconut water in all directions.

The cycling record required a cyclist to run a bicycle for as many hours as possible, without alighting from the cycle for food or for attending to nature's calls, so as to match or break the record about the cycling time that had been established in the other lanes. That time, in every winter season, the unverifiable information about the incredible records established in some or other lanes would be in circulation, in all the lanes of Girgaon; such information and rumours were easily believed and made a topic of discussion, mostly among the children.

By an evening of the first day of the event, the lane would assume a festive air by virtue of a bright light of three or four large bulbs, a sound of songs played on loud speakers, and a crowd, ranging between thick and thin, of the spectators. The first and second days would pass insignificantly, but by the evening of the second day the face of Rashi would appear to reflect the weariness and fatigue; he, however, would continue to stick to his cycle and peddling. Intermittently, Rashi would be seen talking to Appa, who would be walking alongside him, with an air of a general on the battlefield, wearing a shirt and pants, because in those two-three days of festivity in the lane Appa used to dump his everyday dress. Rashi would be found sticking to his cycle till the midnight approached and children at homes in the lane would have already been asleep. Next day morning, no sooner did the children get up from the bed than they would charge to the balcony to look into the lane, which they would find as quiet as a cricket ground appearing long time after the thrilling match was over. Appa would be seen engaged in the daily chores of his workshop, wearing his regular dress of a half pants and banyan. The children would learn from the elders that Rashi had given up the attempt in the midnight as a fatigue had been unbearable for him after the incessant cycling of forty hours; the number of hours of cycling accomplished by Rashi would be lagging considerably behind the record hours heard to have been attained by the cyclists in the other lanes. However, for several days to come, it would be discussed among men and the boys of the lane as to how the oddities hampered the Rashi's attempt to create a record, which, in fact, how capable he was to create.

Appa one day slapped a boy from the lane for a trivial reason, and out of an air of arrogance, without knowing whom the boy was. The boy went home crying and telling his parents about the incident. It was not appropriate for parents to go to Appa, at that time, for asking an explanation or lodging a protest because Appa was as fearsome to any family man of the lane as he was to a person of weaker power, moreover, the outcome of approaching Appa was a foregone conclusion, which would have been the verbal abuses, swearing, and challenges. The uncle of the boy, who was slapped by

Appa, happened to stay in 'Sarkari Tabela', which was then a formidable lane to pick up any trouble with any of the persons residing in that; the uncle of the boy had been on better terms with the gang members of the lane that he stayed. When the father of a boy from our lane approached his brother, with a tale of woe of the boy, he in turn approached the *Dada* of his lane, which was Sarkari Tabela. The *Dada* took that as a personal challenge and prepared his gang at once for an attack on the arrogant and delinquent members of the lane that the brother of his cohabitant stayed. The same night the gang from Sarkari Tabela barged into our lane, at 10 o'clock, challenging Appa by his name. Appa already had a whiff, about the approach of the gang, from some quarter, and therefore he had confined him, along with the family, in his shop, locking the door from inside. The henchmen of Appa, who would otherwise have come at the slightest provocation, were not to be found in sight, for it was as difficult for them as it was for Appa to fight back and pick up a rivalry with the then formidable gang of Sarkari Tabela. The doors of the shop of Appa were repeatedly kicked and struck, with iron rods and hockey sticks, by the visiting gang members for a considerable space of time; thereafter, the gang receded, inflicting severe warnings on Appa hidden behind the door. As per the custom of that time, Appa and his gang were considered to have surrendered to and accepted the supremacy of the challenging gang, once they, in their own lane, had not responded to the challenge of the attacking gang, and they had not come into the open for fighting the attacking gang back. From that day, Appa was thoroughly a changed person as he and his gang had been humbled in the open, and in the precise lane, where they were feared by one and all for their reign of terror.

The Appa's gang members, who were much younger to him, soon parted their ways with Appa. The fear about Appa vanished rapidly; soon, we began perceiving the precocious boys talking fearlessly to Appa, and, sometimes, even scoffing at him. The domain of terror of Appa, in the lane, stood shattered so.

Appa, thereafter, however, remained confined to his old habit of heavy boozing, especially at night, where after he was seen rolling about on the footpath, in front of his shop, with his back to the coarse surface of the footpath. But except that, by then, Appa was more or less a subdued and normal man, with the age beginning to show distinctly in his mien.

But an excellent time for Appa was yet to approach. An Appa's brother had a life jacket manufacturing unit in the dock area of Mumbai. The business was fairly a profitable one because firstly it lacked a stiff competition and secondly it required a skill that was inherently and exclusively prevailing in the caste that Appa belonged. At length, the brother of Appa died; his sons were not interested in pursuing the business, as, by that time, they had been well educated, by virtue of an acquired affluence, to carry on with that business. Naturally, the nephews offered the business to Appa; Appa had no reason to decline the offer because his own business was torpid and his grown up son was not showing any spark in the studies. Appa promptly closed his former business, which was not able to satisfy even the basic necessities of his large family, and joined the new one with a renewed zest and passion in life; the people in the lane began noticing Appa going to C. P. Tank, in the morning by 8 o'clock, to catch a bus going to the dock area, in his changed attire consisting the bush shirt, pants, and pump shoes.

Soon, leaving the school half way, Appa's son joined him in the business. The financial condition of Appa began improving noticeably in no time, but Appa's life style remained as it had been, for Appa was habitual with his old ways and he had no inclination to change over to the new. The Appa's daughters had a fondness for education, they studied well, and one of them even earned a degree from the university; they were duly married in the course of time.

Many years passed, Appa, in the meantime, had not been having any problem in life, and the problem for the residents of the lane from Appa had vanished long ago. Appa, shortly after his power had been shattered, had relinquished his position of a chief of the miscreants of the lane; his erstwhile followers had crossed the age of criminality and had become tired, feeble, withered, or dead, over a period of time, due to excessive intake of drinks and drugs, and because of the lack of a regular income for them, as they had long lost the character and attitude required for undertaking any gainful employment. That time, if Appa and his erstwhile followers came face to face, and there were many occasions like that in the same area, they would not show on their faces, even a sign of their intimacy of the earlier time.

After few more years of smooth life, Appa died in the mid of 80's. The people of the area genuinely felt sad about the death of Appa, because they found a significant existence, in the lane, meeting its end in the death of Appa.

BAPPA KAMERKAR

Bappa was not residing in our building, he was not staying in our lane or anywhere in Girgaon either, but he often came to Girgaon to visit his brother in law, who was staying in the nearby lane. Bappa and his brother in law, which meant the brother of his wife, were freedom fighters of pre independence era. Bappa's brother in law had flourished in the business, after the independence of India, through his dexterity and hard work. By the 60's, brother in law had become quite a rich person, by that time he had two shops of his own, and he had taken three more shops on the rent basis to run a business of selling betel leaves, chewable tobacco, and betel nuts, which was a traditional business of the caste to which he belonged.

It was told by one of the relatives of Bappa that, in the frantic and tumultuous days of the '1942' movement Bappa and his brother in law along with two or three relatives of them, about their same age, happened to go to Ratnagiri and partake in a protest march organised by the congress, they were caught by the British and put in jail. As the district administration had become sluggish and loosened because of the on-going 2nd world war and an impetus of the movement, Bappa and company overstayed in jail, though their presence there was not warranted by any authority. No sooner the jail administration realised its fault than it released the unwanted prisoners, but not before making them eligible, in the later years, for the exalted designation of freedom fighter, by virtue of their stay of more than a required number of days in jail.

In the beginning years of the independence, people of the type of Bappa and company were not looked at with any extra respect or admiration for their scanty, and offhand participation in the freedom movement, for there were many in the society like them and the people of their time knew what actually they had done for the freedom, which, in fact, was a tiny contribution in comparison to the sacrifices of many persons, who had spent many years of their life in jail.

In the year of 1972 India celebrated its 25th year of independence and the term 'freedom fighters' began gaining an archival and historical significance. By that time, many older freedom fighters of the substance had left the world, for the period of the freedom struggle had been spread well over 50 years before 1947; the remaining lot, like Bappa and the company, was fortunate to have a chance to bask in the glory of an exalted position.

The government, in the year 1972 and then, declared many benefits to the freedom fighters, like the reservation in educational institutes and jobs for their children, the pension scheme, and the houses at the concessional rates. The brother in law of Bappa got him allotted a large house in a prominent area of Mumbai by virtue of his wealthy position, for he was capable of paying the margin amount that was required to pay for availing the benefit. That made Bappa sulk by him, and he became more jealous about his brother in law. Later, Bappa, however, could manage to get him allotted a small room in one of the eastern suburbs of Mumbai that he stayed till he died.

From the beginning, Bappa was jealous about his brother in law. He seemed to think that after spending time in jail together they should have continued to live together in all matters, in life, like that of the business, income, and so on. As his brother in law was achieving financial success in the business and earning rightfully by himself, Bappa would take that as an act of selfishness of his brother in law. He was expecting his wife's brother to be more and more helpful, financially, to him and his family. To others' he would say scornfully about his brother in law, who, in fact, was helping his sister's family in his own capacity and means; Bappa was not satisfied with the amount of support furthered by the brother in law, he was considering that support as an eyewash for the relatives.

In Mumbai, Bappa was earning his small remuneration by way of doing the jobs of accounts writing in the small shops, lying here and there, of his relatives. Bappa could not continue with the job at any one place for a long time because of his grave temperament, which had overtaken him mostly because of his failure in life than anything else. He would look at the world disdainful and speak contemptuously with everybody including the children. His light jokes would hold a strange meaning; to a child, found at home on a school day, he would ask whether his female teacher had delivered a child that he was at home. His expressions on the face would be a strange mixture of a mockery and mischievousness. His speech would be full of irony and never be a straight.

He had a small frame and slight structure; he had a flat, pug nose, and his face would look as if it were pressed between the chin and forehead. He used to wear the spectacles, whose quality would not be better than what is distributed, for free, in the eye camps.

He was a congressman by compulsion, his off—hand connection with the freedom struggle would not let him to abandon his allegiance to the congress, moreover, fear of losing a protecting shelter of the respect, which the people had in their mind for the congressmen of that time, would not let him to forsake to be a congressman. He usually used to wear a Gandhi cap, but, getting bored with the cap, sometimes, he would be spotted without it. Firstly he was wearing the clothes made of the *khadi* cloth and he was always found clad in a *khadi* pants and a *khadi* shirt, but, soon, as the first few enthusiastic years after the independence were over, he switched over to the clothes of the synthetic materials, for the *khadi* clothes would look shabby without the starching and ironing, which was a cumbersome and expensive procedure and a deterrent for continuing with the *khadi* clothes.

Soon after the independence, Bappa settled his family in one of the smaller places near Alibaug as the cost of living there was suitable to his meagre and irregular income, and he began working in Mumbai, switching over from one job to another. His poor and hard-working wife, however, accepted the challenge of maintaining the family and began earning by taking the sewing jobs and selling the household items to the villagers in that small place. Sometimes, Bappa used to visit his family and spend some days there with them, without being of any financial support to them in the meantime. Bappa did not contribute anything much to the progress of a newly born nation, only he helped the nation to keep the flag flying high in the world for its rate of population growth. In pursuance of a son, he fathered many daughters and kept the family growing; a son eventually appeared, but not before accomplishing a divine mission of causing many mortals, prior to him, to see the light of the world.

Whenever Bappa would come to Girgaon to his brother in law, he used to visit our home, without fail, and inquire affably about my father and other members of the family. He had a long standing attachment with our family, since the time of my grandfather. I did not know why but he would always remember and mention of my grandfather, who had been dead for long, with respect and reverence.

We had one alarm table clock in our home, which was exceedingly useful in our family that there were many children going to schools, colleges and for attending to some or other events. Moreover, the table clock was made to serve a purpose of the wall clock by way of placing it in a small wooden case that was fixed on the wall at a level at which a wall clock should be. Many times, Bappa used to mention about that table clock in the conversation, he used to say that, he had bought the clock at the request of my grandfather, for which, he would add, my grandfather had paid him the necessary price. It seemed he had developed an emotional attachment, out of memories, with that table clock. Once Bappa requested my father to lend him that table clock for some days, for he had been residing in a place of the relative, where he was required to wake up early in the morning. My father gave him the table clock for using for some days, despite the inconvenience that the family would have been subjected to. Bappa did not return the table clock for several months and children at home began complaining about the persistent inconvenience caused because of absence of a table clock from home for a long time. A Message was sent to Bappa, through a person in touch with him, requesting him to return the table clock as early as possible. Bappa did not respond in words, but one day he went to a workplace of my father and returned the table clock to him. My father, on seeing his visibly annoyed look, took him to a nearby restaurant for having a cup of tea. Bappa was furious and gave my father a piece of his mind, in a friendly tone, for making insistent demands for the return of table clock. On an offer to keep the clock for some more days, he said, in a reconciled mood, that, he had already purchased an alarm table clock for Rs. 9 which at the Kaka's (my grandfather's) time had cost only Rs. 1.75. When I grew up I could visualise the matter in a new perception that Bappa wanted to keep the clock with him, due to his emotional attachment to it, and return my father a newly purchased clock, which, in the meantime, he had only inquired about the price but not afforded to buy. He lied to my father that he had purchased a clock, but, ostensibly, he had only inquired about the price that turned out to be not suiting to his pocket.

All of the Bappa's daughters were married to the eligible boys before the mid 70's; though the marriages were simple and inexpensive they were caused to happen only because of a financial support given by the brother in law of Bappa. By that time, the son of Bappa had grown into a big boy; he soon completed the secondary level schooling and earned his S.S. Certificate. On request from his uncle's family, I took Bappa's son, for he was about my age and new to the city, to I.T.I., and helped him to secure an admission for a draftsman's course. He completed the course successfully and secured a job in one of the engineering companies in the eastern suburb. His job could bring an appreciable financial stability in the family, especially in the advanced age of Bappa and his wife. After the experience of some years, Bappa's son got a job in one of the middle—east countries; the job of son in the foreign country improved the financial condition of Bappa and his family to a considerable extent. Bappa was staying alone in his room, in the eastern suburb;

he began having a decent amount of money sent by his son. Bappa got an itch of lending the money and earning a decent profit by way of charging a usurious interest. He began lending money to the pedlars, road side petty businessmen, and even to some miscreants, in the greed of earning more money in a short capital, and a short period. His tongue had been caustic from the beginning and it became more caustic while dealing with the needy poor people, especially in the bids of recovery of loans and interests.

One day, by the end of the 70's, there was a public function in the building that Bappa was staying, and most of the people in the building were on the ground floor, where the function was held; only the old and invalid persons, who were not able to partake in such functions, were in the rooms. At that time, some persons surreptitiously murdered Bappa by hammering a metal rod on his head and slitting his throat. It was never known whether the murder was committed by a single person or by a group of persons, whether it was pre planned or happened in the heated moments. The police closed the fruitless investigation after some days and the people of Bappa also did not follow the matter further. It, however, was murmured in the area, at the back of the police, that the murderers were the defaulting debtors that grabbed a chance to eliminate Bappa and the debts, at the same time.

In retrospect, many different angles of Bappa's personality and life become perceivable to me; it was not that Bappa was not kind to the children, though his style of jesting was little awkward to interpret for them; as far as his approach to the world, in the beginning, was concerned it can be deduced that he had become a little contemptuous in his outlook because the success was eluding him from the beginning, but, thereafter, he was forced to continue with the same outlook by an attitude of the people toward him that they continued to look at him with a prejudiced mind-set, finding a contemptuousness in his every behaviour, deed, and word; Bappa, perchance, might have contributed to the freedom struggle more than what his relative had told, and his adherence to the congress party might have been genuine and attained out of his participation in the movement in a bigger way than what the people told; his jealousy toward his brother in law might have evolved out of a lurch that Bappa was put by him, or because a business partnership might have been denied to Bappa by his brother in law, despite an expressed or implied assurance given.

Bappa, a freedom fighter, was pitiable in his conditions for which nothing but his grave temperament, contemptuous outlook had only been responsible. I still remember the face of Bappa, which had become how doleful when his son was weeping and telling him about precarious financial conditions at home in the village.

BABA

Baba was the brother of Baa, who was a widow owning a house in the building that we were staying. In the 60's, Baba was staying in the house of his sister along with his two children, an only son and an only daughter. Baba's son was a smart and smiling boy, and he was showing immense interest in the cricket, but his passion was confined to watching and listening the cricket better than playing the game; he would take an extra interest in collecting and safekeeping the old sports magazines, the publication of which was decidedly limited in the 60's, unlike in these days. He had a habit of cutting the photos, concerning the game of cricket, from newspapers and magazines and sticking them neatly in the notebook, like some persons do that in case of the postal stamps. He was an average student, in studies as well as in other activities, at the school. Baba's daughter was a short, peg nosed, featureless girl, and she was in the habit of frowning her brow, when speaking; she was going to school, but it was evident that she was not able to show even a minimum progress in the studies, she, however, continued going to the school despite her failures in the examinations in the intervening period. Baba's wife, whom everybody called Babi, was staying, for most of the time, in the native village of the family, in Goa. Sometimes, she used to come to Mumbai to stay with children, and after staying for 6 to 8 months, she would go away as suddenly as she had come. She was a small and thin lady, and in the beginning of the 60s she was in her 40s; she used to betray boorish expressions on her face, and while standing and talking to anybody she always used to move her upper body in all directions, after a fashion of the creeper.

Baba was a music teacher by profession. He used to give tuitions in singing, and in playing the harmonium and the *tabla*. The people of the area were curious about the Baba's students, whom they would regard in amazement as to what they actually had to do with the music that they were attempting to learn. Besides a few male students, Baba's students were mostly the women, who used to stay in areas as far as Lamington Road, Grant Road, Mugbhat Lane, and who were, by virtue of their family traditions, the concubines of the men of means. When those women were overtaken by a fancy of learning some music for the limited purpose of their occupation they used to search and find a teacher like Baba, who was dabbling in that field for his bread and butter, and who had a minimum required knowledge of music, which he was ready to impart for a small compensation. Baba used to go from place to place for teaching his students, in their homes. On one or two occasions Baba tried to call a student or two to his home for giving them practice in the musical instruments chosen by them. For some time, residents of the building could notice the fair and plump ladies, with the strange expressions on their face, coming to Baa's house to get lessons from Baba. But, the boys from the building, peeping from the door every now and then, began putting both, a teacher and the disciples, in an embarrassing position; Baba soon wound up that arrangement and resumed his daily chores of visiting the homes of his students.

Baba had an average height and a slight body; he used to back comb his partly greyed, greasy hair, which used to suit his clean shaven face that resembled a lion without the mane. When talking he used to waive his right hand in the air as an eccentric godly man does. At home, he used to wear a *dhotar* and a banyan, but while going to the homes of his students he would additionally wear a shirt, and a cotton coat that was as old as the years passed since he had first worn that in his young age. He used to betray the expressions of a whimsical person, and he would be a taciturn for most of time, after a style of the maestro; he was expecting people to regard him as a renowned musician. He never used to talk to anybody on his own, and the people around did not have any reason to talk to him on their own; sometimes, however, when he used to get bored with his perpetual bearing of a maestro, he would suddenly deliver the pleasantries, with folded hands and an idiotic smile flashing on his face, to any elder met on the staircase or in the gallery on the second floor of building; a sudden change in the behaviour of Baba, at the first, would make the recipient of the pleasantries suspicious of him, but the recipient of Baba's pleasantries would reconcile with the situation soon and respond to him by chewing some words in the mouth before he proceeded to his home or work. Baba did not hold any kind opinion about the boys of the building, including his own son, for they would either avoid talking to him or talk to him as if he were a stupid person. Baba, for the reason best known to him, was unnecessary and unusually stern with his children, especially with his son. His son, as soon as he was past his teenage, attempted to commit suicide, on two occasions in a quick succession, by drinking a bottle of pesticide of a famous brand of that time; he, however, survived the attempts, but, in the after effect of his attempts, the boys from the lane began calling him after the name of that famous brand of the pesticide, such chaffing from the boys of the lane, however, deterred him from attempting the suicide anymore. When the son of Baba was brought from the hospital he used to remain lying on the bed placed opposite the door of his house, should the children peep into his room he would smile profusely at them, lifting his head from the pillow. He was a lovely boy, but the sternness of a financially hopeless father, in the age that he was unable to stand on his own feet, apparently, led him to undertake that drastic step of attempting the suicides.

Visibly, the income of Baba was a measly income; he was not expected to receive any handsome fees from his students as they had undertaken to learning from Baba only because they were required to pay a paltry amount of compensation to him in return.

Baba was infamous in the building for his habit of frequently visiting the toilet, which was common for the four families on the floor, and consuming the time therein, more than that any normal person does. There was not a single person on a floor who was not put in a quandary by Baba at the door of the toilet. A thumping on the door of the toilet, in a request of an early vacation of the cabin, would not be taken likeable by Baba, and, ultimately, after an intolerable waiting when Baba used to appear at the door of the cabin the thumping person had yet to hold on to his patience until he received a piece of Baba's mind in the saintly words of him. Besides the habit of frequently visiting the toilet cabin, Baba also had a habit of puffing the *bidi*, which used to accompany him in his reverie in the toilet cabin.

In his later years, Baba took to a fancy of learning the violin, which he would practice in the gallery of his sister's home, but the practicing tunes of the violin created by Baba would be heard throughout the building. Many a repetitive tune of primary nature would be monotonously heard in all the houses of the building; some mischievous persons in the building would say, 'listen, Baba has begun wailing'. After some days, it was perceived that Baba abandoned the idea of pursuing the violin, ostensibly because he could not foresee any progress in the accomplishment of his cherished desire.

By the mid 70's, Baba became fed up with his depleting income, for the creed of women that Baba could find his students began getting more and more interested in the men marrying them than keeping them, and in the new conditions of life they did not find a place for the art that Baba was teaching them. One day, which he had decided beforehand, Baba packed all his instruments of music and other belongings and left forever, along with his children, for his native village in Goa. Before going, he, however, went home to home in the building, where he had passed more than 25 years of his life, bidding a goodbye, with the folded hands, to everybody. It could be perceived that Baba's eyes were moistened while leaving the place that his absence was not to be felt by anybody.

Afterward, it was heard that Baba's son got a reasonably decent job in Goa, but later, in his early 30's, he, unfortunately, died a natural death. Thereafter, whatever happened to Baba, Babi and their daughter were not known to anybody, for Baa would not show any interest in the subject of Baba, if touched by anybody.

MAI AND BAPU

The boys, varying each time in number, from our building would gather, whenever they had an opportunity to pass the time, in the gallery on the second floor, which was the only common gallery in our building what provided an ideal meeting place for the children of the building. Over there in the gallery, the boys used to have their regular chit chatting and jesting or, sometimes, a carom board was arranged, and a game used to go on incessantly till an opportunity was given, turn by turn, to every willing participant. Sometimes, a game of cricket with a ball, made especially by inserting a crumpled newspaper in the discarded socks and sewing the opening of socks coarsely with the help of a needle and the thread, was played in 15 feet by 3 feet passage, in front of Mai's door, between the stairs ending on the second floor and a wall. The ball thus made was hassle free for playing in the passage, without inviting any anger from the elders, for such a softball would neither break any glass-pane nor hurt anybody, even if hit hard.

When the boys were not playing and only chaffing, jesting and talking the mischievous nothing, Mai would enter into the gallery from her home, approach the railings, and begin looking, by herself, into the road below, feigning inattentiveness and without paying any attention to the talks of the boys there. Seeing Mai in that position, feigning ignorance of the surroundings, the boys then would be talking among them about some imaginary fight in the nearby lane, imagined having happened just some time ago; one of the boys would pretend to be a spectator of the fight and give elaborate details of the fight, which, in fact, never had happened. Mai's ears already would be in the conversation of the boys, but she stealthily would listen to as many details as possible, controlling her eager desire to interfere into the conversation. The boys knew, through their previous experience, about the degree of curiosity that such talks raised in the mind of Mai, they would carry on adding to the details of the fight that had been not. Ultimately, Mai, unable to hold to her control, would ask about some details, which would purposely have been held back by the boys in the conversation in order to bring the curiosity in Mai up to the brim. For some time, the boys would pretend as if they were deep into the conversation and consider the Mai's inquiries as if had not been heard by them. That would continue for some time, and, at length, Mai would make her feel contended with whatever information she got out of the overheard conversation of the boys, and she would proceed to perform her next preferred mission of spreading the news. Mai would enter into some home in the building, where she would be welcomed, at that time, without any reservations; she had known, through her experience over the years, as to which house to enter at what time. Mai would be followed slyly by the boys up to the door of the home that she had entered; thereafter, the boys would take such a position that they could overhear the conversation in the room that Mai had entered. As soon as the preliminary exchange of pleasantries was over, Mai would present her dossier on a fight to the members of visiting home; she would talk about the incident, overheard by her, as if it had been witnessed by her with her own eyes, using the first person style of narration. The boys would be amused to see the details with which their original, false story was embellished by Mai; that would continue for sufficient space of time and the boys, after a long moment of self-control, would burst into a loud laughter, which would attract the attention of and amaze all the nearby persons including Mai; others, but Mai, would be puzzled about the cause of a great amusement for the boys.

Delivering and collecting the information to and from every corner of the area was an incorrigible and stubborn habit of Mai, which would anger a few persons, but delight the many. Even a victim of Mai's habit would not stick to the enmity, which would have been temporarily developed after any matter affecting him had happened, for a long time, he would reconcile at the earliest moment because the joy that he would get by knowing the facts of another, would certainly be more in proportion than a pain that he would have got by the divulge of his personal information to others.

Mai had one more habit, which was ancillary and supportive to her first habit that has already been referred to; she was in the habit of slyly entering into anybody's house in the building, at any time of the day; after entering any house, in such a manner, she would be in one spot, making every effort to keep unnoticed for as long as possible, and gather, in the meantime, as much information as her eyes and the ears could tap; the target house would be different from time to time, depending on the contemporary, stimulating trouble prevailing in any house.

Sometimes the slanderous activities of Mai would go too far, and it would happen so that the complaint would be made, by the aggrieved family woman, to Bapu, the husband of Mai; upon such complaint, Bapu would inform the complainant that he would make Mai straight, and he would even scold Mai, in no uncertain terms, in front of the complainant; in that case, Mai would plead 'no guilt' but not retort or say any harsh word to the complainant; after the complainant had left the house of Mai, the high pitched voice of Bapu could be heard from their house for some time. After a day or two, the complainant and the accused, however, would have no worry in exchanging the pleasant words, when they faced each other in the building or at any corner of the area.

But for her habits as detailed, Mai was warm and loving to every child from the building. She was a tiny old lady of a delicate posture; she used to wear a nine yard sari, and her forehead was always adorned with vermilion, of crimson colour, neatly applied in a round shape as large as one rupee coin of today. Mai's features were pleasant, and one could perceive that, at her young age, she had been a petite, good looking woman. Mai was from Malwan region of Maharashtra, and she always used to communicate in no other language than 'Malwani', a dialect spoken in Malwan, unaffected by the language in which the other person responded; but as Mai was simple and unassuming in her nature, nobody used to care for the language barrier and a conversation would continue, without any perceivable hindrances, for the required duration of time.

Bapu and Mai had three daughters and two sons, all of whom, except the youngest son, had been married and happily settled by the mid of the 60's. The youngest son of them died prematurely, by the end of the 60's, without marriage.

Bapu was working in the post of a *Mukadam* (a supervisor) in a civil works department of one of the government hospitals in South Mumbai. Bapu was seen, in the morning by 9'o clocks, going towards Bhuleshwar for reaching his workplace; while going to his hospital his clothes used to be a khaki half pants, reaching up to the knees, which was a part of his uniform, and a half sleeve shirt of any colour, not being a part of his uniform, tucked in the pants; he used to hold a small, flat leather bag pressed under his one arm. Sometimes, Bapu was seen in his full khaki uniform, especially when he used to come home for lunch on any afternoon. Bapu had an average height and a hardy body that was slick and slim; his thin and soft greyed hair, purposely grown at the backside, would be found slightly rolled up at the end, and resting on the nape; Bapu's facial features were delicate and his face used to cast a loving and warm smile, which only the children could recognize, when he came face to face on the road or in the building. Bapu was a happy family man, but he was somewhat tough while dealing with his own children, they, however, used to give him a proper respect.

Besides being a conscientious and dependable employee of the hospital, he was skilled in painting the Ganapati idols and he had a creative hand, especially in painting the eyes and precision parts of the idols; he used to do that job in the Ganapati idol workshop, of his friend, in Fanas *Wadi*, only out of his intimacy to the art and without accepting any money; his only compensation, which was rightfully granted to him, would be a pretty Ganapati idol, for his own home, made by Bapu himself with his own hands, in the workshop of his friend. Bapu would start going to the Ganapati idol workshop from the mid of June. In that period, Bapu used to come home from the hospital by 6 o'clock in the evening, and, after having his dinner by 7.45, he used to leave for the workshop; he used to work in the workshop till late in the night, return home well past midnight, and go to sleep immediately afterwards so that he could rise by 6 o' clock in the next morning for going to jobs in time; the days and nights, in those three months prior to the Ganapati festival, would be of an ecstatic joy for Bapu.

The elder son of Bapu was an artist like him, and he would attend the workshop with Bapu on some days, more regularly in a month preceding Ganapati day. Bapu, on some days, would urge me to accompany to the workshop to see the idols in the making, and if I agreed he would instruct his son to bring me to the workshop as Bapu had to start early to attend to the work. After having dinner by 8 o'clock, Bapu's son would call me, whereupon we would proceed to the workshop, it used to take only ten minutes to reach the workshop from our homes. In the workshop, Bapu would be found immersed in the work, going from one idol to another with a brush and a palette of colours in his hands and attending to only an intricate part of each idol, which required exceptional painting skill, for Bapu was an expert in micro painting work and his hand had an artistic flair; in the workshop, Bapu was to be found only with a thin towel wrapped around his waist and a half sleeve *sadra*, tinged with the various colours, on the upper part of his body. When Bapu saw us, he would greet us with only a warm and happy smile on his face, and ask his son to help me around the workshop and show all the idols, which would be in the various stages of the making; Bapu's son would do the needful more enthusiastically and lovingly, pointing, with a lucid explanation, to each remarkable idol in the workshop. After that, I would be seated in one corner of the workshop, which gave a broad view of the ongoing artwork that would be going on there at that late hour of the night; in between, while the artists had their periodic doses of stimulants in the form of tea, I would be offered a cup of tea, which I would deny or take on the insistence of somebody. After sufficient time, by 11 o'clock, I would begin feeling sleepy and dozing; on perceiving my sleepiness, Bapu would call his son, who would be lending his hand to a job on some idol, to take me home. Soon, walking on the silent road, lit by the street gas lamps exuding a soft, mystique, greenish light, we would reach home; as soon as I lay on the bed I was rapidly overtaken by a deep, sound sleep and sent to a region of dreams, which, in that night, would contain nothing else than the various Ganpati Idols, floating in the background of the sky of the vivid hues.

Come Ganapati festival and Mai would be exuding with the enthusiasm; the house was cleaned with extra care, the walls were painted, the furniture was polished, and shortly thereafter, the first day of the Ganapati festival would appear. Bapu would not be at home till the afternoon of the first day of Ganapati, for he would be absorbed in the workshop all through the previous day and night, he might not have come home even for the food. The younger son of Bapu was given the task of decorating the front room that the Ganapati idol was to be seated for the next eleven days; the boys in the building would be enthusiastically helping him in decorating the room.

In the workshop, Bapu would be extremely busy in giving final touches to the various idols, as per the last minute wishes of customers, and his own idol would be lying in the corner, requiring the work that might be much more than merely a finishing touch. By 2 o'clock, the crowd of the customers at the workshop would become thin, and Bapu would turn to his own idol, sending a predetermined message home beforehand. By the time

'Ganapati' was brought home it would be 4 o'clock, and as soon as reaching home Bapu would go for taking a bath, the preparation of which would have been made by Mai, with an extra care. In the meantime, an idol would have been perfectly set at the place with the help of a mutual consultation, then Bapu would appear in the room, attired in the *Pooja* ceremonial clothes, and the idol establishing rituals would be begun by a *bhatji*, who would have been waiting for long. By the time the rituals were over and people sat to lunch it would be 6 o'clock in the evening.

The Ganapati idol in Bapu's house was always marked for its exclusiveness, every year it would be different, in every aspect, then that was established in any home; year by year, the idol in the Bapu's house had been excellently shaped, exclusively painted, and remarkably styled. The crown of the god's idol was embellished every year by way of fixing it with the semi—precious stones of brighter colours. Even after the 'Ganapati' idol was established at home, on many occasions in the subsequent days, Bapu would be noticed watching the idol, by himself and from a distance, with an artistic perception.

An idol would be carried on the head, from the workshop to home on the first day of the festival and from home to the seashore (Girgaon *Chowpaty*), for the purpose of immersion, on the last day of the festival; the Bapu's idol would be exceptionally heavy and to convey that, on the head, a man of immense strength was required. Only Vitthal was a capable and strong man at hand for performing that task, and every year he would come to Bapu's house at a specified day and time for carrying the idol on the head to the destination.

Vitthal was an employee of the hospital where Bapu was working; he was a subordinate of Bapu. Though Vitthal was working under Bapu, he had developed the intimate relations with the family of Bapu. He used to affectionately call them Bapu and Mai, even though Bapu was his boss in the service. Vitthal would attend to some homely duties of Bapu, not because Bapu was his superior but because he had developed an affiliation with the family of Bapu. Vitthal was a trusted assistant of Bapu in the service, and that was perceivable when the boys in the building had a reason to go to the hospital of Bapu, along with his son, for bringing the bamboos required for making the *kandils* (the paper lanterns), on the eve of Diwali festival, for every home in the building; Vitthal, on the visit of the children at that time, used to give them the choice bamboos in as much quantity as was sufficient for making the kandils for each home of the building. Vitthal was a stout, strong person with almost a black complexion, he had a broad chest and his height was medium, he was always seen in a khaki half pants and a blue half sleeve shirt, which, in fact, was the duty outfit for him. He was staying in the quarters provided by the hospital, in its precincts, for the workers. Vitthal had a boozing habit, which was established in the workers of his type, and boozing was almost a necessity for the type of jobs they were doing; by virtue of his boozing habit, Vitthal was always found with the bloodshot eyes. Vitthal used to appear in our building, in the Bapu's family, on two or three occasions in a year, and every time, whenever he came, he would not go unless he visited our home, inquired of everybody, and jested with the children; it was surprising that the children had never been afraid of Vitthal despite the frightening countenance that he had, on the contrary they were found liking the chaffing and jesting nature of his as they do in case of Santa Clause.

In retrospect, though I do not get the reasons but all the members of 'Mai and Bapu' family used to behave affectionately with me; their elder son would take me to the 'Ganapati' workshop as mentioned earlier, and some time to watch a stage play or a cricket match; their younger son would give me a book to read for two days, each time, when he brought that from the library, and sometimes take me for listening to the songs on the playing records, paying 4 Annas per song; their daughter would teach me to draw a *Rangoli* and give me the *Rangoli* colours when required; Mai would give me a little amount of sweet on my palm, whenever she met me while coming from the temples, and took me to faraway places like Wadi Bunder, Mulund, where her relatives were staying.

Mai was remarkably agile and brisk in her movements, and she could be met in any part of Girgaon, at any reasonable time of the day. Once she met my mother on the way, when my mother was going to the home of a reasonably rich relative of ours for attending to the *Haldi-Kunku* ceremony, Mai inquired with my mother as to where she was going and expressed her desire to accompany her, my mother acceded as it was a ceremony where all married ladies were to be welcome and respected. In this ceremony, ladies smear each other's forehead with a pinch of turmeric and vermilion, thereby wishing each other a company of husband till the death overcomes; the host distributes presents to the guest ladies in their felicitation. When they reached the venue and settled, the arrogant host, perceiving an uninvited guest in Mai, asked my mother, pointing at Mai, whom that woman was and who invited her to this ceremony. That was an insult to a married woman on such an occasion, which was marked for their adoration. Mai did not take the matter in mind and did not say anything about that, after the form of her mental frame. As a fate that it could be called, Mai lived a full life and died while her husband was still alive, and that offensive woman is still living with a widowhood of more than the forty years behind her.

In the 70's Mai was still active and would go all alone to far off places like Kurla, Mulund and Wadi Bunder for meeting her daughters and other relatives, however, in the first years of the 80's, she began becoming weak and shrivelled and could be seen walking slowly to the railings of the gallery on the second floor and standing there for quite some time looking over, by herself, on the road; she seemed to have been thinking of her previous active days. Mai, before long, became too weak, and Mai's family shifted her to their native place for convalescing; there, she, however, died before three months could pass.

Bapu retired from the service in the beginning years of the 70's, thereafter, he had a financially secure situation because he was receiving a pension, though of a paltry amount, every month. However, soon thereafter, he left going to the workshop, in the 'Ganapati' idol making days as his hands began shivering, rendering him useless for the art, for which he was known. Bapu had a paralytic attack by the end of the 70's, when Mai was still alive; we could overhear the bickering, amounting to little quarrels, between the elderly husband and wife, on the point of being helpful to each other, on any one occasion or another, for which each of them was not able. After an attack, Bapu was sometimes seen limping to some nearby places around the lane, but, thereafter, he soon became incapable of leaving home. For the next few years, he was seen sitting in the gallery, for most of the time, and smiling, contorting his facial muscles, when his eyes would meet with the others; his smile would have the same affections, what had been in an earlier time, but then it would seem to have mixed with the shade of supplication.

Bapu, soon, became a problem for the family, and, sometimes, it could be seen his son, at the instigation of his wife, scolding him in the gallery; Bapu would be found listening to son's verbiage helplessly and with a piteous face, without even trying to give any reason to him. At length, Bapu was shifted to his native place as Mai had been shifted before her death, and there he died, in a short time, as Mai had died. The death of Bapu occurred within two years of the end of his wife.

DAGDOO MAMA

On the first floor of the building, that we were staying, there used to stay one man, who had settled in the space under the staircase leading to the second floor and whom everybody called Dagdoo Mama. Any newcomer to the building could not pass the first floor without noticing Dagdoo Mama, and unless feeling watering sensation in the mouth, for there in that space, Dagdoo Mama was seen with a heap of tamarind before him; the sour odour of tamarind would be engulfing the entire first floor and reaching even the ground and second floor of the building.

Due to the favour from the previous building owner Dagdoo Mama had acquired a permit to occupy that space for doing his job in the day time and also for sleeping there in the night, his other requirements as to the bath and the toilet were taken care of by the common water tap and common toilet in the opposite building. After the ownership of the building changed the hand, in the late 60s, the new owner, especially his sons, tried to drive Dagdoo Mama away from that space, but the entreaties from Dagdoo Mama and a promise of his to vacate the space when required by the owner halted their efforts. The owner could not think of making any use of space and Dagdoo Mama continued occupying that space for some more years. The tenants of the building had no complaint about Dagdoo Mama, on the contrary his being there in the night-time used to serve the purpose of a security guard for the building; when Dagdoo Mama used to go to his village, which plan he would declare and publicise well in advance for the notice of every family of building, the tenants would feel insecure and uncomfortable till he came back; the absence of security cover, especially in the first few days of his absenting from that space, was acutely felt by the residents. The first floor passage of the building was isolated and would remain dark in the night, for only one family was staying on the first floor, and the ground floor was occupied by one small eatery, which used to get closed by 10.30; thus the ground and first floor of the building used to stay devoid of any vigilance in the night; in the dark of the night, but for the occupancy of that space by Dagdoo Mama, any anti—social person with a malicious intent could stealthily crouch in that space on the first floor. On the night, the absence of Dagdoo Mama would bring eery look to the first floor; the existence of Dagdoo Mama in that space was exceedingly essential and useful for the security of the tenants of the building; the tenants, however, were never found expressively mentioning to Dagdoo Mama about his usefulness for the security of the building.

Dagdoo Mama used to sell the tamarind balls, that was his small business by means of which he used to earn little money to support his family in the village near Satara; he used to buy tamarind from the wholesale market, tamarind so bought was then made into big balls of saleable weight, but before making tamarind balls Dagdoo Mama used to put lots of labour in cleaning tamarind thoroughly and kneading that with an addition of salt; Dagdoo Mama used to sell those balls of tamarind going to the homes of the regular customers and also walking through the streets, yelling as he walked as the pedlars do.

There were only a few families staying in the building, and all were almost on the equal financial standing, but Dagdoo Mama, I did not know why, used to respect my father the most or rather he used to expressively respect only him in the building; he used to call my father a *sheth*, meaning a wealthy person, though, in reality, my father was not that wealthy as to be called a *sheth*, but that was a way of Dagdoo Mama of expressing the respect; he also used to call me *barke sheth*, meaning a small wealthy person, I used to feel ashamed, but pleased at the heart. If Dagdoo Mama had any problems or any complaints he used to come, neatly dressed and wearing a *pagote* (an oversized head gear made of the long cloth), to my father and tell him about his current woes as if my father were the owner of the building; my father used to give him a patient hearing, along with a cup of tea served by my mother, which used to alleviate Dagdoo Mama's woes, and he should leave with his half worries vanished.

Dagdoo Mama was above 55 in the mid of the 60s, and he had been staying there in that space, in the building, at least for 25 years before that, meaning he had come there when he was in his youth. When I used to see him, he was a man with a medium height and hardy body, his complexion was dark, and his face was withered, his facial expressions would oscillate between the kindness and the peevishness, his movements were slow but sure. Dagdoo Mama used to clean—shave his head at least three times a month, and every time after having his head clean shaven, from his usual roadside barber, he would be found sitting bare bodied in his place, wiping his head and body in his peculiar slow movements. Once, an idiotic servant of our family was sent to a flour mill with an instruction to bring flour as soon as it was done because there was some urgency at home. The servant came hurriedly with an open container of freshly ground flour, which was hot as it was turned out of the mill only a few minutes before. He came up to the first floor and stumbled on the railings in such a way that the whole of the hot flour was spilled over the just then clean shaven head of Dagdoo Mama, for Dagdoo Mama's barber had left a few minutes before after completing his job, and Dagdoo Mama had settled down to the task of wiping his head. Because of the sound many people in the building, especially the children, gathered on the first floor, only to find Dagdoo Mama standing in a state of agony with his full black body coated with the white flour. The children had a fabulous time watching Dagdoo Mama, for some time, in that embarrassing condition, but soon they took to their heels, for Dagdoo Mama should not feel offended. As expected, the next day Dagdoo Mama came to our home to meet my father and rebuke the servant with the help of *sheth*.

Once there was a guest in one of the families of the building, he had been in that house for some days since; the guest had not noticed the existence of Dagdoo Mama in the early days of his stay in the building because Dagdoo Mama had gone to the village before the guest came. It so happened that on that particular day, in the evening of which Dagdoo Mama had returned from his village, the guest had gone to another relative in the suburb to dinner and he was late in returning to our building; as he returned to our building it was 1 o'clock in the night, and as he came to the first floor passage he saw a black figure making slow movements in the dark. The guest, it was clear, took Dagdoo Mama to be a ghost and went running the second floor staircase in the strides; he did not tell anybody, lest he would be considered a coward, but left for his village by the first mode of transportation available on the next day morning, at the time the guest left the building Dagdoo Mama was away from his place, possibly for taking a bath or attending to a call of nature, in the toilet of an opposite building; having reached home the guest wrote to his relative that there was a ghost on the first floor of the building which he had a chance to encounter the previous night of his departure. The guest's relative in our building did not send any explanation for an apparent reason.

In the last years of the 60s, one new family came to our building as a tenant, the boys in the family were grown up and quarrelsome; they did not like Dagdoo Mama respecting and having rapport with the older residents of the building, in comparison with them; even the boys' mother, who was a stout woman, would encourage the boys in harbouring enmity against Dagdoo Mama; the boys began picking up the quarrels with Dagdoo Mama and talking to him as if he were an errant boy, other residents of the building could not explicitly support the side of Dagdoo Mama, for he was an encroaching person, and not a legal tenant, and was residing there without even a support of the building owner; Dagdoo Mama's position became precarious, besides the building owner had also been waiting for a chance to evacuate Dagdoo Mama. On a casual request from the lane's 'Social Service *Mandal*', which request was instigated by the quarrelsome boys opposed to Dagdoo Mama, the owner allowed the *Mandal* to make a small wooden cabin in the space that Dagdoo Mama was settled, for keeping the instruments used in the sickness.

After the displacement, Dagdoo Mama still continued for a few years, staying in the small strip of space where the staircase from the ground floor to the first floor ended. As Dagdoo Mama tried to stick on to place the incidents of bickering, however, increased. Dagdoo Mama got tired of the quarrels, and by that time he also had grown older to withstand the hostile conditions; the affable conditions that he had passed his years in the building had faded away with the passage of time. One day, in the beginning of the 70s, he declared his intention of a permanent departure from the building and also from Mumbai; soon, on one day, after meeting all the good residents of the building, Dagdoo mama left the building and Mumbai, where he had stayed for more than the 30 years of his life. Thereafter, Dagdoo Mama was never seen again, and nothing was heard about him.

MANMOHAN

Manmohan used to come to our home along with his aunt, who was employed at our house for performing the sundry jobs, like washing clothes, sweeping the house, and cleaning the vessels; it was the time of early 60's and that time there was no dearth of the workers, who would do such jobs, as it is today. The servants of that category were easy to find at a payment of monthly salary, which used to be surprisingly low at that time; such workers were found to be employed in most of the families in Girgaon; the servants of that type used to perform their jobs with utmost sincerity and with a sense of belonging to the family, for which they worked, so much so that they used to become a part of the family and participate in all the events, happy or sad, of that family, as any other member of the family would do.

The aunt of Manmohan was an old lady, whom we children called *Aaji*, meaning grandmother, though my mother used to call her Damuchi *Aai*, meaning mother of Damu; Damu was the son of her. *Aaji*, as I think now, was not as old as what she was appearing to be. She was a little, shrivelled, thin, dark complexioned woman, and she always used to wear a mild, pitiful smile on her face. She was a widow and had become so not at a late age of her, which generally was the case with many women from the poor bracket of the society, of that time, that she belonged. Damu was the only son of *Aaji*, and she never brought Damu to help her in the work, as she was doing in case of Manmohan. Sometimes, she would bring Damu with her, but that was only when there was an occasion to send through him some eatables or advance money, which used to be primarily for his self-purpose.

Manmohan was to share the food with his aunt at home; *Aaji* used to get home the left over, which she was collecting from our home, as well as other homes that she was working; besides that my mother would give Manmohan some food, when perchance his aunt was not about, which he used to eat as fast as a famished dog does.

At that time, Damu was a boy of 15 years, and Manmohan was about the same age of him. Manmohan, who was a son of *Aaji's* sister, was brought by *Aaji* to Mumbai to stay with her, after he lost his father and mother, in the village, in quick succession; he was 5 years old when he was brought by *Aaji* to Mumbai; Manmohan, however, soon reconciled with the new conditions, after a habit of a pet brought home.

Manmohan, though a poor and poorly looked after a child, was chunky in appearance. He had a slight Negroid features, and his hair was thick and wiry, but his complexion was of wheatish colour. While helping his aunt in her work, he would steal a time, in between the work, to look after me and to partake in my playful activities, which I needed, off and on, as any child of that age does.

Over a period of 5to6 years, *Aaji* grew older, and she was not able to attend to the work, she stopped working in spite of her desire to continue. Moreover, Damu also had begun to earn for the family as he had got a job in the illegal country liquor joint run by a local blackguard, from the creed of the *Dadas* of that time. Manmohan continued with his aunt for some time, but, soon, he, as a grown up boy that he had become by that time, set him on a lookout for any 'all and sundry' job, which his ignorant mind and an able body could do to get him a bread and butter. Manmohan, it was clear, was not a literate, but his body had grown into an able bodied young boy, who as if had been fed and looked after with a great care by his family. It was obvious that Manmohan had taken care of his own nourishment in a manner that he was eating in our home, out of the warmth of my mother; apparently, he had tapped many such kind hearts here and there.

It was a period of the early 60's and that time the construction work of 'Sahitya Sangha Mandir' (a drama theatre in Girgaon) had just begun on the big area in Kele*wadi*, where, before, the Marathi dramas were played in the open air, and before that it had been a disused burial ground of any religion that the dead bodies are buried. The digging for the foundation was undertaken on a remarkably wide field, and the digging was going deeper and deeper in order to match the massive structure of the proposed building. Manmohan, in the meantime, had found a menial job for him on the sight of the said construction.

Even after she left our job, *Aaji*, sometimes, would visit our home, out of an affinity, and so would Manmohan. One day, while he was on the digging job, Manmohan came to our home, in the lunch recess, sneaking away from the job. He was betraying the mood of secrecy on his face and he had assumed an air of being on some important job. He had with him one parcel by his side, which was wrapped in such a dirty and worn out cotton sheet, which, once upon a time, could be of a white colour.

After an initial suspense, Manmohan finally opened up the issue in a low secretive tone, darting his glances in and around the room and at the entrance door of our house. He told my mother that he had brought something that was particularly helpful for the well—being of the family, he also added that the people were willing to pay any amount for the things he had brought, which would cause an ample luck to the family that possessed it; he also added that it was not easy to get that thing unless a luck favoured any family. Observing the amount of concern exhibited by the face of Manmohan, my mother also got engulfed with the equal amount of anxiety, and she hurriedly told him to show that mysterious thing at once. Manmohan, at length, opened the parcel, which laid the strange things before the eyes of everyone present there; on seeing what the bundle contained, my mother became stupefied and stunned for some time, but, soon, reconciling to her senses, she shouted at Manmohan and sternly ordered him to pack up things and leave the house immediately, for the things that Manmohan brought in the bundle were a skull and few bones of the human body, which, ostensibly, he had obtained from the site by digging. Manmohan got confounded on encountering exactly the opposite reaction than the expected of my mother, he could not know what that exactly irked my mother, but he began packing the things, murmuring the rueful words, and left our house. While he was leaving my mother warned him, patronizingly, never to be on an errand like such to this house in the future. How a mother could withstand such things in the house that was full of children. My mother, however, could perceive earnestness and ingenuousness in the Manmohan's intention of bringing those horrid things to our home, and that was evident in consideration that she gave to him on his next visit.

Since the beginning Manmohan had some feminine traits in his features, behaviour, body movements, and facial expressions, but when he was in his childhood his those traits would blend in his child worthy manners and make him more likable as a poor, innocent child; the elders would consider him with a warmth and sympathy, and for children about his age he would be an enjoyable buddy. But with the passage of time, Manmohan naturally grew into an able bodied young man, and with that his feminine features became intense, pushing him to a boundary of a eunuch personality. Manmohan was aware of the anomalous state of his body and mind, but he could do nothing more than accepting the existence, without regretting, as it was given to him by the nature. The people of the area had begun to regard him as a eunuch—a *chhakka* or *hijda*-, and his previous world was in shambles before him, for the people began either avoiding him or attending to him, in case of any need of them, in an evasive way as if he were afflicted with a dreaded, contagious disease.

Aaji had already shifted to her village in an emaciated condition, soon we heard that she died there of a pneumonia. Damu, as said earlier, was in the job of a salesman—*bechanawala*—in a prohibited country liquor joint, but, before long, there he took more to consuming the booze than to selling it. Resultantly, Damu soon fell ill with a liver malfunction and lay huddled in his room for some months; in due course, he sold his room for a few thousand rupees and shifted his abode under the staircase of a *chawl* that his room was. The cash received by Damu, from selling the room, vanished in a short period, as quickly as camphor evaporating in the open air. Within a few months, Damu's condition worsened, and he was shifted to a government hospital, where he died after some days. 'Dada'-the boss of Damu—was kind enough to make him to the government hospital with as much promptness as one could show in throwing a half dead rodent out of the house. Dada also exhibited his kindness and generosity in arranging the funeral of Damu; the funeral was arranged in such a haste that it could match only with what had been shown, in the previous days, in case of the persons dying of the plague. The funeral procession was arranged with all the paraphernalia, which was considered especially necessary in the strata of the society that contained the likes of Damu; the funeral procession was accompanied by the *Bhajani Mandal*, and as the night was approaching the men carrying gas lights on the head were called for. It was monsoon season, and it was drizzling when the procession began. The mysterious green light exuding from the gas lamps on the head of carriers, the chorus songs sung in a melancholy tone by the *Bhajani Mandal,* with a strange music in the background, and the drizzles in a falling night—at all, the atmosphere became so miserable and frightening and produced such a gloomy effect that it made a little crab crawl in the heart of every child present there. The funeral procession was preceded and succeeded, besides in between, by an ample supply of the country liquor, out of the benevolence of Dada. For many days, thereafter, the local residents remembered the procession more than they did Damu.

As for Manmohan his past relations were extinguished, and he was left with no relations, worth counting, to fall back upon; the past world of him was already devastated long before. By this time, he, however, had found for him a new world that his real but lately surfaced character could find a place.

A small community of the harlots had taken to the inhabitation in the lane opposite to Gai*wadi*, known as Kande*wadi*. The harlots had their houses in the buildings on the either sides of the lane and also in the by lanes. Their houses were surrounded by the white-collared, middle class residents, and in some buildings the usual residents were even residing, though grudgingly, with the harlots in their neighbourhood. Besides the customers of the harlots, the lane also was frequented, in the day time as well as in the night time, by the local *goondas*, for their defensive presence there was required by their pet harlots, and they also had to visit the secret drug joints, in the lane, out of their addiction. In spite of a meek but steady resistance and protest from other residents, the community of harlots obstinately stayed on in the lane; nobody, however, could tell easily since when the harlots had chosen that lane for their habitation.

The lane was also visited by the eunuchs, for they were befitting to work in the houses of harlots, because of the exact nature and body of them; also, the eunuchs were traditionally required by the harlots for taking care of the rituals of their goddess.

Everybody soon found Manmohan frequenting that lane, for he had made quite a few friends for him, from his creed, in the lane. Before long, Manmohan began working in the houses of harlots and, soon, thereafter, he was seen on the road, going somewhere, in a robe of a woman, with a basket, containing the brass deity of the goddess prominently placed in it, on his head. Firstly the people who knew Manmohan and who saw him for the first in that new costume would see each other out of astonishment, but soon it became a habit to their eyes and the excitement died off. Then, that was not surprising for anybody to find Manmohan in that lane, at any time, in any robe, either male or female's; thus began the new life of Manmohan.

Manmohan, once in a while, but more rarely, would come to the door of our home and inquire, out of affinity, about well—being of my father-mother and every of my brothers, without entering the house; my mother would give him a few coins and ask him to eat something out of it. In the first, he would visit the door of our home in the man's clothes, but once he came in a woman's clothes, with a basket of the goddess on his head; my mother gave him one rupee in the name of a goddess but told him in a tender motherly way to avoid coming in that garb to our home, for, ostensibly, she felt that Manmohan's that appearance would possibly affect a mind of children; Manmohan smiled by himself, but, thereafter, the amount of his visits to our home reduced noticeably.

It was the beginning of 70's, and during that while the wedding of my eldest brother took place. The moment Manmohan had a whiff of that he turned up at our door in his, then regular, woman's garb, with the goddess on his head; he profusely blessed the newly married couple; it could be felt easily that the blessings were heartier than professional in nature, and deeper than shallow in the character.

The year after year passed, everybody was engaged in pursuing his own studies, profession or business for achieving a progression in life, and nobody had a moment to think about whatever was happening in the life of Manmohan. Manmohan had religiously adhered to his self-imposed limitation of not talking or showing any association with anybody from our family, when met in the public or on the road, so as to save us from any embarrassment. Whatever information we had of him was from the servant, who was then working on our house and who majorly often chanced to meet Manmohan on the way to a vegetable market in 'Sadashiv Lane', which was near to Kande*wadi*; in every meeting, Manmohan would affably explore with him of everybody from our family. We learnt from our servant that, by then, Manmohan had left wearing the women's clothes; in the subsequent period, Manmohan was always seen in the man's clothes, with his hair grown to the full length like a woman, and his brow smeared with the turmeric powder; Manmohan had grown his hair long like women because that had been a demand of his profession.

After a few months, on one evening our servant casually conveyed us that Manmohan was not keeping well, and he had learnt that from Manmohan himself, when he had met him earlier that evening; none had even a thought to pay any attention to that casual information about Manmohan.

We had a neighbour, an old woman, from the second floor of the building that we were staying, she was called Mai by everybody; Mai was a little old lady but had a remarkable fondness for dispatching and obtaining information to and from every nook and corner of the area. That was a period of the last years of the 80's, and one evening, while returning from the market, Mai instantly came to our home and informed that Manmohan had died, she also added that only a few minutes before she had seen his people taking his dead body for the cremation. Nobody spoke any word, but it was obvious that everybody's mind was shrouded with the strange, sad feelings.

MADHAVRAO

Madhavrao, the name seems to be that of a person from a princely family or a judge of an important court. No, it was the name of our barber in the childhood. Madhavrao, however, was successful in his attempt to keep personality close to his name. He was of a remarkable posture, and an average height, he used to back comb his gray hair, in a style of a drama artist of that time; in fact, we children were given to understand, in the mid of the 60s, that Madhavrao was still some time before then had been acting in the dramas presented by the local drama companies, but we did not have a chance to watch him on the stage, because, by the time, we children came of age he supposedly had stopped working in the dramas; his past association with the stage, however, was evident when he would murmur some songs from the dramas, while cutting the hair, which were not known to us and which appeared to be from the period before the 50s. The reddish tinge in his eyes used to talk about his drinking habit, which was unusually familiar with the drama artists of that time, and his clothes would resemble that of the drama artists, who used to have that dress code in the daytime when they were not performing on the stage and whiling away their time going here and there; in keeping with the style of a drama artist, Madhavrao would always wear a *dhotar* of a superior quality cotton, though that would seem to have been bought at the time when he had been working on the stage; over the upper body he used to wear a silk *zabba*, reaching up to the knees, which, visibly, was more but not less than 10 years old, at the time when we were seeing him in that same *zabba* on every Sunday. When he was seen, from the balcony of our home, approaching our house, in the late morning of any particular Sunday, with his barber's tin bag hung from one hand and his other hand engaged in holding the corner of his *dhotar*, nobody, than those who knew him, could understand that he was a barber coming to our home for cutting the hair and shaving the faces.

Madhavrao was supposed to come to our home on the first Sunday of the month, and he was adhering to the schedule for many years, but in the ensuing years he began coming with an irregular frequency because his drinking habit had begun going too far. Madhavrao used to take advance money, out of his charges, going to the work place of my father, well before the Sunday that he was scheduled to come to our home; on his request my father used to give him some portion of his charges beforehand. In the beginning period, the demand for advance money was restricted to a reasonable portion of the estimated charges payable to Madhavrao for his visit on any Sunday, but as his drinking habit became unrelenting he began going to my father's workplace more often than before in expectation of some or other amount in order to satiate his lust for the drinks; resultantly, the amount paid to him began becoming higher than his charges of one time. Then the plan of Madhavrao, of coming to our home, went awry; he was supposed to come on the fourth Sunday from the last Sunday, on which the hair cutting had been done, leaving three Sundays in between; but as an advance paid to him began becoming bigger than what his onetime charges were he began coming after two Sundays on one occasion and after four Sundays on another occasion, making the children, sometimes, appear as the army recruit boys, and, sometimes, as the inmates of the mental asylum, depending on how much time interval was left between the two hair cuttings. His coming to our home was earlier if the advance taken by him was coverable in the charges of one time, for he would clear the way for the further advance, and his coming was delayed if the advance taken was not coverable in the charges of one Sunday.

His speciality was that he would cut the hair as he wished, without heeding a suggestion or an expressed wish of a head before him; instead of cutting the hair as per the liking or the suggestion of a head bowing person before him he would describe him in small words how the suggested hair style would look awful on his head and not match his face. For the new haircuts of that time he had his own terminology; he used to call the crew cut a 'tin-pot cut' and the soldier cut a 'mental asylum cut', he was not seen cutting the hair of the girls, but the 'bob cut' was named a 'zipri cut' by him. Getting sulked with an attitude of Madhavrao many grown up children began stealthily going to the hair cutting saloon for getting their hair cut, but soon they found that no better skill than that of Madhavrao was present at the saloon, even though the charges there were more by one and half times than that of Madhavrao, moreover, the idea of children going to the saloon was not acceptable for the parents. So the children used to return to Madhavrao for the hair cut, submitting an explanation to him that due to some programme in the school they had to resort to the barber other than him, and that the time was short and a neat haircut was a requirement of the programme; they would offer to Madhavrao their heads for the haircut, which he then would do pressing the nape before him more in the degrees than his usual requirement of the ninety degree angle.

Surprisingly, Madhavrao would dismiss the requests for his service from the other residents of the building, even if they asked him to visit on some other days of the week than Sunday. He would come only to our home because of the previous acquaintance of him with our family. He did not like to pose as a barber before the others, who would look at him merely as a barber, without being aware of the brighter side of his personality; and, in fact, in our home he was treated affably as a family barber, my mother would inquire with him about the well-being of his wife, whom she knew, and his children; on the eve of Diwali festival, he would be given a packet of homemade sweets to take home for the family; on some Sundays he would be given the mutton curry and *chapatis* to eat, because by the time he finished the hair cutting of my father it used to be a lunch time at our home. Funnily, after finishing the job in our home, he used to take to shaving his own face clean, looking in the wall mirror, before the dish of food was given to him. At the earlier time, when he was perfect in the accounts, he used to linger on in the hall of the home till the time my father finished his lunch and came there, he would then, in the low tone, account for the amount receivable, get some money, and go.

On one of the Ganapati days, he used to bring his wife to our home, on the insistence of my mother; his wife was a woman of the village background and did not suit to the personality of his, his sons were also of a simple background, and even though they were going to the school they did not seem to be competent for a serious pursuit of the studies; the poorness of Madhavrao was conspicuous in the clothes of his wife and children.

In the late 60s, Madhavrao became more addicted to the drinks; moreover, he began turning out incapacitated for the brisk movements, which was the necessity of his profession. His frequency of going to the work place of my father, in an inebriated condition, for an amount of money increased day by day and eventually he was required to be told, in the stern words, to mend his ways. Soon, Madhavrao began coming more infrequently, avoiding many Sundays that he was required to come; moreover, the number of heads submitting to him for the hair cut reduced day by day because the grown up children began preferring going to the hair cutting saloon, avoiding Madhavrao. By the beginning of the 70s, Madhavrao totally stopped coming to our home.

Madhavrao's brother Dattu, who also was in the same occupation by tradition, began coming to our home in a bid to take over the customers of his brother; Dattu was no match to the personality of Madhavrao, he was a boorish person and was always to be found wearing a white *lenga*, and a shirt, with a 'Gandhi' cap on his head. In the matter of the skill of hair cutting, he was lagging in the previous decade. In the changing time, Dattu could not be accepted, as a barber, in our home with the growing children; after a year or so, Dattu stopped coming to our home for cutting hair, and there ended a system of the family barber at our home.

When Dattu used to come to our home, in the first few years of the 70's, we would hear from him that Madhavrao was not keeping well and moving out of home; as informed by Dattu, Madhavrao's sons had begun working in the same profession, and were earning for the support of the family, the financial position of the family had become better than at the time that Madhavrao only had been earning. In the mid of 70s, Madhavrao died in his home in Mumbai, and that was what we could learn later of Madhavrao, from one of the common acquaintances.

NANITAI

There was one woman, who was staying in our neighbour and who was called Nanitai by everybody. Nanitai was a divorcee, and she was staying along with her only daughter, who was about 14 to 15 years of age in the early 60's. Nanitai, in fact, was not our permanent, real neighbour, for she was staying, in the problematic years of her life, in the house of her well to do elder sister, who had a large family. Nanitai was a primary teacher in the municipal school, even though she was not a highly educated woman; in those days, when Nanitai had joined the job, qualification of seventh standard passed had been sufficient qualification to secure a job of primary teachers in a municipal school. Nanitai was a thin woman with a medium height, and her posture was as straight as a stick, she had the pockmarks on her face. At the first, the children would not be inclined to like Nanitai because her appearance was not as pleasant as to attract the children to her, but, once the children had a chance to spend some time in her company they were overtaken by her kindness and loving words, and they soon would begin getting attracted to her and liking her.

Because of inevitable bickering in the big family of sister, due to the Nanitai and her daughter's existence in it, Nanitai soon shifted her residence to the home of her poor brother, having a considerable number of daughters. Nanitai was staying in the house of her brother for quite a few years, however, before long, she was allotted a residential quarter by the municipal corporation, and she shifted to the new residence along with her grown up daughter; Nanitai was staying in the municipal quarter till the time she retired from the service.

In the building that we were staying there was one family, which had many school going boys. The financial condition of the family was reasonably OK but not strong, and it was inevitable because the father of the family was the only earning individual and the boys were still going to schools and colleges for completing the studies. In the mid 60's, the eldest boy of the family received an appointment letter, from the government bank, which, however, contained a precondition of depositing the security deposit of Rs.500/, before joining the service; the time available for fulfilling the requirement was only 7 days. The job, evidently, was so potent that it would have changed the financial condition of that family for better and helped the younger boys in their pursuit of education. The family was in a quandary, as raising such a large amount at such a short notice was not an easy task in those days. A fairly well to do and close relative of that family, when requested for the loan, demanded a promissory note against a loan of 500 rupees, that did not go well with the pride of the parents of that family and therefore the demand was turned down at once; such a disrespectful demand of the relative of that family, it was obvious, was backed more by the jealousy than a principle. The problem reached the ear of Nanitai as that was common in the way of life of that time; Nanitai, on her own, went to the mother in that family and told her, '*Vahini*', as that woman was called by that name by everybody in the building, 'why do you worry when your son is getting such an admirable job; you should enjoy, in fact; and as about rupees 500/ you leave the problem to me, I have a rotation of the loan available to me from my credit society, I will avail the loan and give you the required cash, you pay off the loan in a period of two years, which, surely, will not be a problem for you'; there was no reason for the mother to deny that angelic help, which, as it was proved over the time, served well for the future of her sons.

When Nanitai was staying in our neighbourhood, she used to take the elderly children, about the age of her daughter, from our building for the school picnics, which she was required to accompany as per her duties. The parents had no problem entrusting their children in the safe hands of Nanitai, the question of the safety of the children, itself, would not occur in anybody's mind. In that way, on some days in the 'Diwali' and Christmas vacations, it would be a plan of Nanitai to collect as many willing children as possible from the building and bring them to one of the gymkhanas, which lay on Marine Drive on the West side of the railway line between Charni Road and Marine Line railway stations. The programme would be decided and conveyed by Nanitai a day or two before; on a prescribed day, the children would gather at the gate of the building; as soon as all were gathered together, the group would begin proceeding under the supervision of Nanitai to the gymkhana, the route to the gymkhana was like, come to J. S. Road, which was just about 100 feet away from our building, take a left turn and reach Thakurdwar, take a right turn at Thakurdwar and reach the walkover bridge at Queen's Road, cross the bridge and come to the aquarium, from there take the left turn and the gymkhana would be in sight; the entire journey would not take more than 10 minutes from home. On seeing Nanitai and company approaching, the gardener of the gymkhana, working in the distance, would come running with a welcoming grin on his face. Nanitai had developed a close relationship with him during one of the sporting events of her school on that ground, and contact had thickened during the course of time, for which the nature of Nanitai had only been a contributory factor. The children would be in a delighted state of mind because of the outing in a pleasant morning in October, November or December; their minds would be refreshed in no time by the openness of the ground, and fresh, salty breeze coming from the sea. Firstly, in the given chance, the children would begin gamboling and running helter-skelter in the open ground, but Nanitai would, soon, gather them together and start the games, which would be played primarily with rubber balls, rubber rings, and oversized plastic ball. Nanitai would oversee the games, play the role of the referee, and check the uncontrollable children. Some grown up children would go as far as Marine Lines Station and take the cycles on rent and keep on cycling in full speed on the ground, up to the fullest enjoyment of their minds, and then they would teach cycling to those, who were eager to learn the same. On the ground, sometimes, Nanitai would get for children the glasses of *sherbet* or small toffees from the pedlars, who would be hovering around, for their untimely business, on finding a small group of children at such an early hour. After more than 2 hours spent in the games and fun, Nanitai would recommend winding up and marching back home; all would gather together and slowly begin walking homeward under the guardianship of Nanitai. The gardener would come running to bid goodbye and wish for coming back soon. The way homeward would be the same as it was for the gymkhana. In between the road, from the walkover bridge to Thakurdwar, there was one *chikki* shop at the rear entrance of Sarkari Tabela, Nanitai would allow the children, those who wished, to buy *chikki* from the shop or, sometime, she would herself get for them. It would be 9 to 9.30 when the group reached Thakurdwar, and it would face many known faces, from the area, hurrying to the bus stops or to the Charni Road Station for going to their workplaces because it would not be a vacation for them as it would be for children and Nanitai.

By the beginning of the 70's, Nanitai had happily settled in her new home, which was a municipal quarter allotted to her; she passed many years there, in the meantime marrying her daughter to a good boy. She retired from the service by the beginning of 80's and began staying with her daughter; the monthly pension being paid to her was sufficient to support her financially, without a need to look at anybody's face for the help. Despite having gone off to stay, she was coming, occasionally, to her sister in our neighbour; in her visits, sometimes, she used to stay in the house of her sister for a day or two, during which time she used to spend quite a substantial amount of time with my mother; my mother used to gain information on various matters from her, out of her experience in the outer world, for she was a working woman of the time that the women were hardly going out of houses to work. Nanitai used to keep real interest in every body's well being, especially in the progress of the young boys and girls whom she knew from their childhood and who grew before her eyes. She passed a contented retired life with her daughter, grandchildren, and in the shadow of affection of many, who had occasion to experience the warmth and consideration of her, before she died in the mid of the 90's.

HE

He was born and brought up in Girgaon, and he stayed, married, fathered children, and died in Girgaon. He was a natural and original *Girgaonkar*. He was born in the early part of the second decade and died in the early part of the last decade of the 20th century. He could be called a true *Girgaonkar* of the 20th century, for he happened to witness and went through all the happenings in Girgaon, in the larger part of that century, as a passive participant or an inquisitive observer. He did not participate in any great movement, in Mumbai, either in the freedom movement or in the '*Sanyukta* Maharashtra' movement. He did not attach himself to any political party, despite whatever frenzy that created in Girgaon around him. He did not, of course, partake in any riots that touched Girgaon, except that he only watched the tumultuous and violent events from his gallery or the corner of some streets and kept him informed fully of the on-going incidents. In a nutshell, he had a detailed record of the eventful happenings and incidents in Girgaon of the 20th century, even though he could not boast of actually having participated in or having an active experience of them. He was not an ardent supporter of any leader or political party or ideology, he was fond of and habitual of only witnessing and recording the events, mostly which had some humour in that; he was an instinctive observer of the happenings, which had been occurring around him.

In the 60's and the 70's and even in the 80's, he would be seen in any part of Girgaon with any dress on him, for throughout his life, he never stuck to a particular dress code. Sometimes, he would be seen in the *lenga* and full sleeve shirt, and at another time he might be found in the snow white, pleated pants with a full sleeve shirt neatly tucked into it; on some occasions, he would be overtaken by a fancy of wearing the thin cotton *dhotar* as a leg wear, and a silk *zabba* on the body; on a special occasion like 'Ram *Navmi*' (the birth anniversary of Lord Rama) he would not hesitate to wear a *pugree*, a headgear of olden days. In one of the old photographs, he was even seen in a dress that the hunters of the British Raj era, when they were in the game of hunting, would wear. His bespectacled—mischievous face, a broken front tooth, and greying hair standing on the head like a forage crop would make him look comical in any clothes that he would wear. His speech was tinged with humour, and he possessed a knack of fitting himself into any group of persons, speaking the language of the time, irrespective of the age bracket what they belonged.

By profession, he was a photographer. He was in that profession from the time when every photographer used to have an assistant by his side, in order to hold a flash bulb stand and load camera, every now and then, with a roll of negatives, the number of which would depend on how much richer the client was. He had in his collection the pornographic photographs, of the girls of a little loose virtue of the A . . . o Indian community or such other communities, which had been shot in pre independence period; he used to claim that those photographs had been clicked by himself on the demand of the girls themselves; he would show those photographs to the lip smacking young people, narrating a juicy tale about an each noticeable photograph. He was working with one of the photography studios in Girgaon, which was owned by a Parsee old man, who himself was a photographer of the period whose technique was almost outdated in the 50's. He used to be in the control of the studio as the old man would leave that to him for most of the time; his generous boss had given him an implicit permission to do photography contracts on his own, besides attending to duties of fulfilling the contracts received by the studio, which used to be mainly about the parse weddings and 'Navjot' ceremonies. On his own, he would take the photography contracts for wedding ceremonies or any such family programmes, mainly in the families of his relatives and friends, that besides photographing the events, he would play the role of keeping the gatherings bursting with the peals of laughter, by means of periodic delivery of the witty comments directing the participants, from which even the hosts, bridegrooms, and brides could not escape. Sometimes, he used to come suddenly to our home at any hour of the day and click photographs of the children in whatever clothes and spirit they could be found, for he would be in a haste of finishing the half used photo roll before proceeding to the place of the next contract. Most of the childhood photos in our family album show the children in the most natural expressions and the barest conditions.

At the time when the technology of colour photography was not invented, he would take to brush and water colours and turn a black and white photograph into a colour one, on his own wish or a requirement of the customer, colouring an old lady with the crimson lips, thick black eyebrows, and black hair, or making the lips and cheeks of a young man or a boy as rosy as if he were born in Kashmir; sometimes, he would make the hair of an aging man as jet black as a crow, making it difficult for a mortal object to believe that it was his own picture. Despite this sort of artistry, his business would be brisk at a time because the people were as much interested in seeing themselves or their loved ones in the colours as he was in exhibiting his crude colouring technique.

As for trick photography, he had his own technique, which he had developed indigenously for his own purpose. He had hung on the wall of his home a photograph of himself that he was seen as a professional body builder with only a vest on him. If any guest, new to his home, alternatively looked, with a question mark on the face, to him in the present and in the photograph on the wall, he would say that, in his young age, he had been overtaken with a craze of body building and had built his body like that; on close observation of the picture, the guest, however, would, soon, find out the trick, which would be discovered to be a painless and basic artwork that involved nothing more than cutting out and sticking the necessary parts of two photographs together before taking a fresh photograph of a morphed picture. On one occasion of a Sankranti day (14th January), which is traditionally a kite flying day, he took out and distributed copies of a photograph that he and his wife's heads were stuck in a place of the heads of a boy and a girl going to the terrace with the kites and a reel of thread under their arms. All such activities, it was evident, he would attempt with a sole purpose of a healthy jest and to bring smiles on the faces of the people, in their otherwise dull and complex life.

On some occasions, an eccentric conduct of him, however, used to shock the children. When he came to their home he would be exceedingly jovial with them, but, sometimes, when he met them on the road, when they would be going to or coming from the school alone, he would turn his face as if he did not see them at all. A child, on meeting the eyes with him on the road, would expect a smile or a word of compassion, a child's expectation, however, would be stumped by a glance, which would seem to have come from an unknown person. Many boys would call him names for his such conduct, but I perceived that he had a right to be serious sometimes to give a thought to his worries, which he might have been hiding behind the mask of his humorous personality.

He had many amusing tales to tell from his life, which he had passed in none other place than Girgaon.

His one tale, which was about an incident, that had happened in the 40's, when he was in his youth, about a passing way through the gutter at the end of Mugbhat Cross Lane made many groups burst into merriment over a period of time. The said lane was a dead end lane, as at the end of it a large building facing J. S. Road had separated this lane from that busy road. After the sewerage system of that time, every two buildings had a gutter provided between them for the residents to throw the litter in that. At the left corner of the dead end of Mugbhat Cross Lane, there existed a gutter which opened on J. S. Road. The residents of the area would pass through the gutter for reaching J.S Road, which they had to visit frequently for some or other work or for going to the bus stops or a railway station. They would pass the gutter, despite a chance of litter spilling on them, because it was the most convenient short cut to reach J. S. Road, moreover, the passing of a gutter was not taking more than 10 seconds. Over a period of time, it so happened that the right of the residents of buildings to throw the litter in the said gutter was overridden by the customary right established by the passers-by, through their everyday usage of the gutter. Resultantly, the gutter would be passed as quickly as possible by the passers-by, so as to avoid a litter falling on them, and at the same time the litter would be thrown in the gutter as stealthily as possible by the residents of the adjacent buildings, so as to avoid any unsavoury words pointedly directed to them from below. Once in the late evening, he was passing through that gutter in his usual routine, and a voluminous litter came on him dirtying his clothes and body. In a fit of rage, he looked up to locate the culprit that dispensed the litter, but she (at that time only women and not men handled the kitchens) had vanished from the window as soon as she dispensed the litter, out of her well cultivated habit, and with a resolution, which also was long practiced, to pay no heed to the verbiage, if delivered, from the gutter below. He was, however, determined to discover the dispenser, and on a spur of the moment he shouted from the below, 'o madam, your silver spoon has come with litter, please collect'. A woman, momentarily forgetting her resolve, promptly peeped out of the window for gaining a silver spoon, which, she was sure, she had not lost and must belong to others and which a shouting person had found. Upon an appearance of a face in the window, he, standing still in a gutter below, immediately delivered a piece of his mind, in his own humorous way, to her and proceeded.

The other tale that he would tell, was from his teenage, and which was a period of the mid 30's. That time the over-zealous heads of the families would go to the Girgaon *Chowpaty*, in the early morning, to buy the fish so that they could please their wives at home with the sea fresh fish bought at a reasonable price. The fishermen coming from the sea, in their small boats and with their fresh catch, would be interested in selling their fish as early as possible, even for a little less cost, so that they could be free for other work or to enjoy during the rest of the day. The buyers would be assured of the freshness of the fish as they could see the fish being brought from the sea right before their eyes. In those days, he, along with his one or two friends, would go to 'Chira Bazar', a retail fish market in Girgaon, in the late evening and buy the fish, for he was aware that the stae fish was available for a dirt cheap price at the closing time of the market. Taking along the fish bought on the previous evening he and his friends would go to *Chowpaty* early in the morning; they would enter the sea with the fish in their hands and having had dressed as the fishermen's lads do. After dipping in the sea for some time and getting sufficiently wet, they would come out to the shore in front of a prospective buyer, targeted from the distant, with the fish held noticeably in the hands. The buyer, on seeing the fish just then brought from the very sea before him, would pounce on the children of fishermen in disguise and immediately strike a deal; the customer would go home thinking how his wife at home would be greatly pleased to see such a fresh fish bought at so reasonable a price. Every time, a transaction could earn him and his friends a rupee or two, which was a considerable amount of time.

In the early 30s, the roads of Girgaon were dimly lit and they used to turn deserted after 8 (o'clock) in the night, after the way of life of that time, and because the population was decidedly sparse. Most of the men of that time would wear a headgear in the form of a *pugree*, *topi*, or *pagote*. He and his equally naughty friend would cower in the darkness of two sides of a lane, with an each end of a string in the each one's hand; when they would perceive any person approaching to pass through the lane they would adjust the level of the string, held tightly, to the level of the headgear of that approaching person; when passed the spot, the person would suddenly find his head gear displaced from his head and fallen on the road; the harried person would collect the head gear hurriedly and take to his heels, lest the ghost caught hold of him.

In his later years, he established the friendship with a pathologist, who was much younger to him at the age; the pathologist's clinic was only on the opposite side of the road. He would spend most of the time of the day, in the clinic, in the company of a pathologist. He used to lend a helping hand in completing the chores of the clinic, and in the spare time they both would have a fabulous time in each other's company, for the pathologist had developed a passion for his humorous company. He added some funny incidents from the clinic in his stock of the humorous anecdotes. He would describe how a person came for a urine test with a beer bottle full of urine or for a stool test with a box full of stool; on another occasion, he would say, how a man was in a quandary and had to scuffle when his semen were required for testing.

He could be the only person in society who had changed his caste on more than one occasion, at least for his own belief, for, in the Hindu religion, it is said, caste would stick to a person as he is borne and leave him not before he is dead. In the first, he was expressing a steadfast allegiance to a prominent caste in Mumbai, then he switched over to a caste free *Varkari* sect and remained attached thereto for many years; in his later years, he established a strong attachment with an important caste in Goa, ostensibly, out of the influence of his friendship with the pathologist, who belonged to that caste. His intention of shifting his caste loyalty, every now and then, was without any serious thinking attached thereto.

He crossed 75 years of his age. His daughters, many in number, were married long before and had teenage children by then; his daughters, sons in law, and grandchildren would come to meet him, and he would tease his sons in law and grandchildren, after a fashion of a young man jesting with his friends. He was a supple bodied from the beginning and was active even in his that age; he still could be seen wandering here and there in Girgaon. The people had no qualm to believe that he would cross a century of his age, and they covertly wished him for so. However, when he was nearing his 80, he suddenly became a victim of an intestinal cancer and died within one year of the detection of the disease. With his death, an informal and entertaining history of Girgaon of the 20th century went behind the curtain.

THE BALUS

In Girgaon of the 60s and the 70s, the domain of household jobs was reined by none other than the Balus, who were people from a farming labour class of the middle Konkan part of Maharashtra. They were so used to wash the clothes and clean the vessels from home to home in Girgaon that it appeared as if they had been doing that job from the beginning of the world and would continue doing till the world ended. Their way of life, their mental set up, and their social structure was hugely connected and interrelated with theirs that occupation in Girgaon.

They would make any area under any staircase of any building as their abode, where they would mix up the food collected from the various homes, eat, sleep, wake up, father the children, feed them to grow to meet the ancestral profession, invite the relatives to dinner, and even keep an eatery to make the customers to enjoy the food of various culinary hands, for an affordable cost.

That while the use of the refrigerator had not yet established in the domesticity of Girgaon. The food remains, left over at almost every home, after lunch, and the dinner of the family members was over, had no takers except the Balus that were working in each home of Girgaon. After the work had finished at a particular home, the food remains (in whatever form say *daal*, rice, vegetables, non-veg curry), which were kept apart in the vessels meant to be taken away by the servant, would be lifted by a Balu and reached his dwelling place before proceeding to another home for doing the job and, thereafter, collecting the food remains from there. The Balus, after every dwelling member had reached the abode under the staircase, would evaluate the likelihood and the ways of mixing the food so collected; one of the members of them, who was active and might have gathered expertise in the task of handling the collected food and distribution thereof, would be taking the lead and decision in that matter of food mixing, he would mix up the material so collected with such a skill that each of the Balus that partook the meal would be left licking the finger even after the food was over; the tastes, that the blending at the hand of Balus created, were hard even to have been imagined at homes, from which the food had been collected. Their sense of blending the food was beyond the conception of a simple mind; they would mix the *daal* with *daal*, vegetables with *daal*, non-veg curry with *daal*, vegetables with non-veg curry and what not. Once the final blending were over than the quota of rice from each home would be gathered in one heap; thereafter, they would begin eating, along with their visiting relatives as well as the customers of their eatery, without uttering a word till they finished the food. The advanced members, as they used to think of self, of their community were working with the wall painting contractors or some shops as a helper; the advanced members would be earning little better than those who were working home to home, but they did not enjoy the privilege of getting the food from any home; such members of their community used to establish a deal with the food collecting relatives of them; the advanced members would eat every day at the place of the food collecting group against a monthly payment of the pre decided amount. The Balus also had some other acquaintances and relatives, who would be working, as the non skilled workers, in hotels, in Girgaon; however, they had not to depend on any of relatives or acquaintances for the food; the reason was obvious, they were well fed at the hotels, where they were working. The Balus were so dependent on the homes, where they worked, for the food that they used to specify that as a service condition, before accepting the job. If, for any reason, the food were not to be got from any home then they would refuse to accept the job, or they would ask for a higher wage than they got elsewhere.

After the mid of 70s, many people in Girgaon began installing the refrigerator in their homes, the number of which increased day by day; this changing circumstances noticeably reduced the proportion of 'take away food' available to the Balus. At the same time, there was one more change in the situation that began shattering the monopoly of the Balus in the household jobs, in Girgaon; it was the emergence of the 'Hyderabadi', locally known as kamathi, community, in Girgaon; Hyderabadis, knowingly or unknowingly, began competing with the Balus in their area of monopoly. The Hyderabadis were more agile and rugged than the Balus and would serve to their duties more systematically and cleanly, they did not require food from the working homes, and they would take the food remains if insisted, out of helplessness; income wise they soon overtook the Balus because they were hard working and they began undertaking additional jobs of washing the cars and the two wheelers in the morning.

Some Balus used to have their wives with them while they were living and working in Girgaon, and both, husband and wife, would do similar type of job, while other Balus might leave their wives back in the village; their wives staying in the village, along with the children, would be earning a little remuneration by way of working in the paddy fields, or growing less costly grains on their mini land holding around their houses, or collecting berries, forest mangoes or Java plums from the jungles on the small mountains around the villages.

It was not so that a Balu in Girgaon, with or without a wife staying with him, would continue staying under the staircase all day through the year, he would go to his village once or twice in a year and stay there for one to three months, aligning his trip with the Ganapati or Holi festival; while going to the village their luggage would include the brooms, buckets, and stack of used clothes collected from various homes, if not more. If the S.T. bus were to leave by 9 o'clock, the departing Balus would reach the terminal by 4 o'clock, along with the crowd, in the proportion of one to four, accompanying them to see them off while the bus left.

After the mid of the 60s, when the small prosperity started showing its face in Girgaon, by virtue of the better jobs of the offsprings of the old *Girgaonkars*, the Balus began bringing their sons or daughters of 10 to 12 years of age for keeping them with some families, on a monthly salary basis; that son or daughter of Balu would stay with family and help the woman of the family with her daily chores of household work, the child would eat and sleep in the same home. The parents of the child would visit the house of employment at any time, along with quite a large number of relatives, overtly to meet the boy or girl casually but covertly to assess the employment conditions and to discover if the child were facing any grievance; during the visit, their behaviour, consisting of darting eyes, tactful questioning, and dedicated mum, would agree only with that of the labour inspector visiting any premises where gross violation of labour practices is suspected. The advance salary for some months would have been taken already by the father of a child at the beginning of the employment. After 6 months or more, on one evening, the father of the child, along with a crowd of the relatives, would visit the house of the employer and declare that he was taking his child to the village in the same night, and so the account be settled immediately. The woman of the house would be in a quandary at the idea of suddenly losing a helping hand in everyday household chores, for which she had become used to past several months since; the father of a working child would not yield to fervent request and entreaties from the lady, or any other member of the house, and even the neighbours, who were kind enough to imagine the precarious position to which the woman in the neighbourhood was subjected to; the father of the working child would face the situation steadfastly and indifferently, uttering only minimum necessary words, and take away the child and the remainder salary, conniving at the sorry faces of the bystanders around. After one or two days, the child would be spotted in Girgaon by some neighbour in the building, and after three or four days more it would be learnt that the child had been kept for the job in the other house, some distance away, ostensibly, after the father having taken an advance pay for six months or more from the new employer.

It was not so that the Balus staying under the staircase would never face any tough situation; sometimes, a hot headed resident of the building, that the Balus had taken refuge under the staircase, might become enraged with any objectionable behaviour of any of them, usually like his having felt that he was not heeded or respected by them like his rivals in the building, he might be seen throwing the scanty belongings of a Balu on the staircase below; a Balu, in that case of a hostile situation, would not respond or obstruct or reply but only put with a sulked face before an enraged resident, the situation would soon be quieted by the involvement of other residents, who would even support a victim cum culprit Balu to gather the strewn belongings together. In subsequent days, the Balu would be more indifferent to the enraged resident than before, clearly indicating to him that he would not get the respect even what that he was getting before. In the event of their coming face to face, anytime in the future, the sulky expressions on the face of Balu, at the time of hassle, would be seen to have transferred permanently to the face of the enraged resident.

A new owner of the building, in case of ownership changing the hand, or a young son of the current owner, would sometime be overtaken by the idea of evacuating the Balus under the staircases of his building; thereafter, for many days, he would be found engaged in the job, which he had been obsessed with, by means of talking to some people in the lane or in the building or the shopkeepers in the building or the occupant Balus themselves; the Balus would be seen feigning some concern on the face, when the owner was about talking, in connection with the contemporary matter, to others or to the Balus themselves. Having not sensed about the exact measures to be taken and about how to face the unpleasant glances from the residents, the owner would soon quit his zestful idea of evacuating the Balus from under the staircase of his building.

Come Ganapati or Holi festival and the Balus, those who had a plan to stay back in Girgaon without going to the village for the festival, would slowly start practicing their *Naman* dances under a staircase of the building, which provided for wider area and where the tolerant people resided. In the beginning, the practicing exercise would be without any musical instruments, but soon, as the days passed, the sounds of the small drum (*dholki*) and the small bells (*ghungru*), along with a heavy thumping of feet, would be heard throughout the vibrating building. When the festivals would appear, the practicing team would go to homes, where any of them was working, in the dramatic costumes; they would produce a dance episode of fifteen minutes or more, in each home visited, making every floor and every house of that building vibrate deliriously; the dances would have been performed on the songs worded and composed, about the cinematic songs of the time, by themselves. They would collect the cash reward, for their uncalled for performance, from the chief of the house and depart for proceeding to the next house, waving hand to every known person met on the way.

After the turn of the 9th decade, the Balus began switching over to the jobs of other types, the generation of the 60s and the 70s of them had already stopped working long ago because they were either old and feeble to work or dead; their children had begun working as an unskilled worker, in the small time companies. The earning members of the next generation of Balus prefer staying in the slums of suburbs to under the staircases of the buildings in Girgaon; many of them are staying in the slums of the suburbs of Malad, Kandivali, Santacruz, Bhandup, Ghatkopar and likewise. Gone are the Balus and gone are the Hyderabadis from the clothes washing and vessels cleaning jobs in Girgaon; now that jobs are being done by the poor and hardworking women of Girgaon, who live in their own homes, and who have got children going to school, and whose husbands are either having a job or out of the job for some reason.

Even now, if you happen to visit your friend or relative staying in one of the buildings in Girgaon, and if you happen to peep in a space under the staircase, you will still find one or two small trunks tucked in the angled corner under the first stair, and one or two clothes hung on the nail stuck in the nearby wall. A few rushes are still clinging to the bank even when the great flood has washed many big-trees away.

A FRIEND'S HOTEL

The father of my best friend, from Girgaon, owned a shop, admeasuring 1500 square feet, on the main road at the corner of Prarthana Samaj. The shop was prominently located on the J. S. Road and was exceedingly suitable for any business. He had been running a grocery shop there since the mid 50's. The father, however, died In the early 60's and, as the ill fortune it was, all three brothers and one sister of my friend followed the father, in a span of one year, in their childhood. The widowed mother of my friend was left with only one son, that was my friend, and one daughter, who was 10 years older than my friend. The mother continued the business only by herself as her son was only a 7 year old boy by then. She ran the business honestly, and because of compassion felt toward her, as she was the widow, by the people her business in the area was brisk and profitable, she ran the business for a considerable number of years. By the mid of 70's, mother of the friend was met with one person, who had dabbled in the hotel industry, and who gave her, and her son, 18 years old at that time, a rosy picture of a restaurant being run in the exact location of their shop; he insisted them to turn the place into the restaurant (hotel, as called in Girgaon), as soon as possible, taking the bank finance, without which nothing was possible to proceed any further. He readily agreed to become a working partner and to make his experience available for the success of the project; he, of course, was not to risk his own money, or to be a party to the loan from the bank. The bank funding was duly availed, and the restaurant was opened, on one of the national days, at the hand of a fairly prominent politician. The business began running, and the working partner was happy to be at the helms of the affairs of the restaurant, at such a prominent place, without having had to put any money into the project. He soon began to impose his own terms, and he was annoyed if any question were raised about any of his decisions or instructions. After more than a year, it was felt that though the business was pretty decent it was not sufficient to service the mortgage on the head of the owner of the place. The working partner sensed the storm to come and began picking more and more points of disagreement. One day, under the pretext of a petty argument, he declared that it was not possible for him to stay connected with the project under the circumstances prevailing then, and he left abruptly and as quickly as possible since he had nothing of his own in the business and he did not have to take care of the winding up of any matter. The mother and her inexperienced son were left in between, by the working partner, to manage the business, which they were not experienced with. The mother, son duo was put into a quandary; they, however, ran the business obstinately for two years, but failed to cope with the rising financial debt; they eventually sold the business, along with the place, for an amount, which was only sufficient to satisfy the bank loan. In a bid to change over the business, the family lost the shop, which is valued at the several crore rupees as at present. I am telling this story since it is concerning my best friend, and it is about an unsuccessful hotel in Girgaon.

'I'

I was born in the beginning years of the 40's. I was born in Girgaon, and till now I have spent the whole of my life in Girgaon; even if anybody offers me a sizable amount I will not leave Girgaon till my death overtakes me; I have an umbilical connection to Girgaon, which I would never end for any price.

I was the only son of my parents, though I had four sisters, two of whom were born before me and two after me. All of us were living in one small room in Girgaon, where I have been living till now; the condition of the room is same as it was 50 years ago, when my father was alive and at the peak of success of his life.

As per my mother, and as she would always tell everybody, I was a good looking lad from my childhood. Having imbibed in my mind from my childhood that I was a sweet looking boy, I have been holding that belief throughout my life. My mother, in my presence, talked so much about my looks, every now and then and to everybody, that I was convinced with the idea that I need not do anything else in life, when I was bestowed with so good looks by the nature, which achieved me adoration without doing anything.

I had a fair complexion and the straight nose and my facial features were striking. Most of the children are adorable in their childhood, but my mother felt that I had an extraordinarily beautiful look, better than any other child. My mother would compliment me before every other mother, who, I remember, would agree with her on her face but laugh at her and chaff about her at the turn of her back. During a conversation, if a reference to any good looking man or a hero of the films were made my mother just would say that, that person, good looking like my son or that hero, handsome like my son. So much praise from my mother and family, in my childhood, gave me the impression that from my birth I had already achieved the recognition and admiration, for which people had to spend their whole life; I started getting overwhelmed with that idea and lost interest in doing anything, even pursuing the studies.

Mother would compliment me, and in turn my sisters, under the influence of the views of the mother, followed the suit. For pleasing my mother or having influenced by the wife's opinion, my father also would do the same praising about me in his talks with others. Other people would not contradict him for fear of developing an adverse relation or getting branded with the jealousness.

My father was working with a clearing agent in the dock area of Mumbai. He was not a much educated man, but by virtue of his good luck in life he was in such a job that would give him an extra income, almost more than five times of the salary that he was getting, though, the extra income had nothing to do with his meagre education. He had cultivated a perception, based on his own situation, that's a good job with an extra income was sufficient for the fulfilment of the parameters of happy and contended life. He would behave with an air of a rich person with the other persons, even with those that were educated and in the good jobs, though their jobs were giving them only salary and no extra income. He held a queer opinion about education and would tell even the educated people, on their face, that, what education had done any good to any person; they knew that his views were unhealthy for the society, but they could not prove that, in view of their paltry salary income coupled with no hopes of generating any extra income out of their current jobs. Because of his station in life, which he had happened to achieve without any valued education but because of sheer luck, he would impose his opinion about education in others; they would listen to his opinion on the futility of education and keep quiet, for they could not prove to him otherwise, off hand, knowing, however, fully well in their minds as to how lethal his views about the education were.

I grew into a boy, and by that time it became obvious that my body would not reach the height of even an average standard. With the growing age, I began remaining shorter than the boys about my age, which, however, did not hinder my mother from delivering the praises in the proclamation of my good looks, even though I had begun losing the tenderness of childhood and becoming a short, stubby boy with the rigid features on the face.

It was not because of my father's views about the education or my mother's excessive praise about me, but I did not find any value in pursuing the studies right from the beginning, I had been going to the school, but only with a sinking heart, for quite a few years, I was studying without any heart into it. As a stream fallen log would be carried to some distance and then thrown on the shore, I went up to the 7th standard and left the studies; however, on the insistence from my close relatives, I continued going to the night school for the next two-three years, that, however, did not help me in making any perceivable progress in the academic studies.

My father was an excessive drinker; he would leave for his job at 8 o'clock in the morning and come home in the evening, by 8 (o'clock), in a thoroughly drunken state, with some notes of 1-5-10 rupees spilling from his pocket of the trousers, thereafter, he would sleep for two hours before getting up to have a dinner, upon eating the dinner he would go to sleep again for getting up in the morning before 6 o'clock. During the time, when he was at home and not asleep, he would talk voluminously that all at home would keep quiet without replying back to him, unless necessary. However, he was not a drunkard of the wretched type; he would gladly welcome the people and relatives at home and properly play host to them; he, in a delightful state of mind of him, even would go to visit the relatives staying in the distant places, taking along his neatly dressed wife and children. My father had two brothers who were staying in Girgaon, in nearby areas; they were better educated and in better jobs than my father; however, they were not as prosperous as my father was, because, though their salaries were better, they did not have any extra income in their jobs to match the means of my father. Their children, however, were showing the progress in studies, in a far better way than I and my sisters were showing.

Despite his pronounced views about the education, my father did not deter me from going to school, but he would not have the morale to scold me should he notice my sluggish approach toward the studies. Moreover, my father's absence from home for the most part of the day, his drunken state when he was at home, and my mother's active role in shielding me helped me to hide from my father my repetitive absence from the school and disappointing results in examinations.

When my father was at the height of his income, he married one of the elder sisters of mine to a young boy from Alibaug, whose family had a reasonably large house built on one small piece of land; the house was built by the family out of the superannuation benefits received by the father of my brother in law, and the family members had been boastful about their house. My father spent a considerable amount of money on marriage, and he was glad that he could get a son in law, who was from a land owning family. We were happy that we found a place, out of Mumbai, where we could go rightfully; we began visiting Alibaug, and in the next few years we had many visits there under the pretext of some or other cause, or just for spending some days in an amusing and elated spirit. After some years, we found that the financial position of the family of my brother in law was not as strong as it was thought to be; my sister's husband lost his job in the district bank, in a few years after his marriage, because of a fraudulent transaction for which he was responsible, and the condition of their family became more precarious. Over a period of time, our visits to Alibaug reduced noticeably in number, but as I was grown up by that time I used to go alone there many times to avail the hospitality and admiration of my sister and her calm and quiet husband, for they used to welcome me eagerly because of my city upbringing, and in order to please my mother and father.

After having spent a considerable amount, out of the savings, on the first marriage in the family, the experience of which was not as savoury as it was expected, my other sisters were left by themselves for finding husbands for them and raising funds for their marriages. They religiously fulfilled the desire of the family, and, soon, found the jobs, suiting their education, in smaller companies, and, thereafter, the husbands for each one of them; after the marriages of all of my sisters I had four places available to me to visit for enjoying the admiration, pampering and warmth of my sisters and brothers in law; I could pass good many days of the year visiting my sisters' homes, some days, every time, with each one of them.

Some scrupulous people tried to find jobs for me, but in each job, which I could join, either my way of life did not suit my employer or the expectations of my employer of I did not suit me; resultantly, I spent many years after joining some or another job and each time leaving each job after some days. Soon, I found myself over-age for jobs in various places.

When I was in the 7th standard, in my school it was essential to choose one vocational subject, which was taught in an extraordinarily cursory manner and the marks of which were not reckoned for the result of the final examination. I had chosen the subject of the watch repairing for that purpose; that subject came handy to me to feign gainful employment when I would be out of jobs, and after I became an over-age for any job worth counting.

My father became ill with a malfunctioning of the liver, and, soon, he left going to work, for he had become incapable of going out of home. He was left with no balance of money off him, and the employment conditions of his job were such that he did not receive any superannuation benefits on his leaving the job. His condition—financial, physical and mental—became extremely critical; my sisters, who were the earning women, would help my mother in that difficult period, without letting me know of support, for I should not feel guilty or ashamed for not having been helpful to my family in its hard time; that much care my mother and my sisters took of me in order to keep me mentally pleased in any case. My father died within a few years of his illness.

My mother's proclaimed appreciation about my looks, since childhood, had made my mental frame so determined to the idea about my good looks that I would seek any girl, whether pursuing higher studies or with a far better family situation, to be my lover and the wife thereafter. I had a strong feeling and a cherished wish that any girl, of a rich father or with an education to earn a substantial salary, would accept me, most wishfully, as a husband, I expected them to have longed for me. I was in search of a suitable girl of that type, and I began casting nets at every probable girl, who would fit to my desire. There were many dreamy girls around, whose dreams, in that age, were confined only to a romantic relationship with any young boy with an acceptable feature; I would throw a net on one or more of them at a time. In that period, many suitable girls got entrapped in my net and dreamt with me, when together, about the romantic life in the future; it continued for some period, but, thereafter, all girls, however, escaped the net in a short period of time, either because they regained their senses in time or their fathers sensed about the non-sense dreams of their daughters before the time was lost. I crossed my 35 years, and my design about the female company of my dreams began shattering; I came across a casteless, unattractive girl, who was a reasonable educated girl and earned an average income from her job with the cooperative bank. My growing age and hopeless future forced me to prefer an unattractive dame to a beautiful girl, and an earning girl to a daughter of a rich father; my long cherished wish was frustrated and that extinguished my passion of wallowing in the richness of a father of a beautiful girl.

When I got married, I had almost reached my 40 of age. After my marriage, the financial position of the family, however, became steady because of a small income, received every month, in the form of a salary of my wife. Besides, due to the employment benefits available to my wife, I and my wife visited some distant tourist places of interest for the first time in my life. My wife, soon after accomplishing her ambition of acquiring a reasonably respectable family name, began keeping secrecy about her income and bank balance, and she began spending only as she wished; she, however, was taking care of the bare minimum requirements of the family, whereby she began getting a control over my old mother, who could do nothing but the cooking food. I decided to reconcile with the conditions for the sake of peace in the family, and because I could do nothing else in the matter. As far as my own expenses were concerned, I was left to earn by myself. Over a period of time, my aging sisters had become busy and engrossed in their own families, with the growing children therein; they would not have the time or charm to adore me or show hospitality to me. After two years of marriage, at length, my wife gave birth to a son; I was extremely happy in my heart, but I did not have the resources to celebrate my joy; hence I remained reticent.

After a birth of son, my wife's world was limited to him and her job, which was particularly valuable to her to earn an income for the up-bringing of her beloved son. My role in the family began becoming more and more irrelevant, for which, however, I did not care; I let my wife bring up her son the way she liked, and take any decision about him the way she wished.

Some ten years passed like that. I had curtailed my requirement to the bare minimum so that I could control my spending to my paltry income from the sundry jobs, which I had been undertaking for many years. My nephews—my sisters' sons-, who were the earning young boys by that time, would occasionally give me some money in token of love, which I was happy to receive. I am an occasional drinker, my nephews have been sometimes giving me a small bottle of whisky, on receipt of which I would get overwhelmed by their love toward me; such acts of the young boys make their mothers happy, I think they gift me with money or whisky bottles for pleasing their mothers instead of I.

After I had crossed mine 50, I came across a time that I could have some income of my own. My brother in law from 'Alibaug' has one cousin brother, whose family, in the first, was exceptionally poor. My brother in law's cousin could carve a place in the district committee of the ruling party of Maharashtra by dint of his dexterity, cleverness, and hard work; by 50 years of his age, he became a name to reckon with in the district, and as well as in Mumbai, because that time he had the close contacts with many ministers in the state government. He is about my age, and I had a friendship with him from the time my sister came to 'Alibaug' to her husband's family. I began going to the 'Mantralaya'—the secretariat—and even to the various police stations, mentioning the name of the cousin of my brother in law; I found that his name would make a miracle and any work in conspicuous places of government would be done without any difficulty. Many people, who came to know about my newly found ability, would come searching me for getting done their work at the police stations, or some or other department of the state government. I would also go to the builders (the professional building constructors) taking some or other complaints of the persons, who had suffered at the hands of them. In undertaking all such types of works, my intention, in the beginning, was about doing the social work, but soon I learned that people pay for such a service and that they do not pay unless it is asked for. At length, I acquired a knack of getting the work of the people done and making sufficient money thereby. At the spread of a word, the people began coming to me for getting done their some or other work, which had stuck in an administrative quagmire or which required a mention of any important name for that to happen. Having perceived that people even pay some amount in advance, I began demanding money from them as soon as they came to me with some work. I received the advance money for many works, most of which even did not move an inch further. Before long, it became my notion that it was not required to do the work even though the advance money was received; I received a fair amount of money from many persons, who would follow me, for several subsequent days, entreating and drawing my attention to complete the jobs soon; I began enjoying the prominent and influential role assumed by me, and treating the people carelessly and arrogantly. At length, some complaints reached the ears of the cousin of my brother in law, upon which he became furious thinking that his name was being spoilt by my deeds; he castigated my brother in law, who in turn reprimanded me in the harsh words. The cousin spread a message in the necessary places, and the officers, who were welcoming me in the previous, began driving me out at the first sight; a source of my substantial income was cut off abruptly. A few generous souls did not follow up for the refund of the advance money, a small number followed up for some time and left the attempts after they got tired, but the others were exceptionally strong and did not leave me until their amounts were refunded; that way I lost the name and the money earned. By that time, I had crossed my 60; my mother left the world shortly afterwards.

I knew that I was not respectfully welcome at the social gatherings, functions, and in the houses of the relatives because of lack of education and income of mine. To overcome that situation I inculcated a habit of visiting the houses of relatives that are in distress, due to illness, hospitalisation, or death in the family; I had known by experience that in such condition anybody, whoever is useful in some or the other way, is accepted, invited, and welcome.

My son has grown up into a young man, he is a well educated boy, he was blameless in the studies for which the hard work, support, and care of his mother had only been instrumental; he has joined a decent job, and he earns a decent salary, which he gives to his mother, who takes care of all his needs as she was taking there-before. My wife has retired from the service and got her hefty superannuation benefits; she is receiving the pension every month, albeit I do not know about the figure of any amount received or being received by her. My son married a lovely girl working with him in the company, where he is working. My wife, along with my son and his wife, has shifted to a newly bought flat in the western suburb, but I refused to accompany them as I do not want to leave Girgaon in any case; they, however, did not insist much for my accompanying them. The life is going on and on, and I cannot say that I am not happy with the life.

The 'I' in the above narration is still living in Girgaon. He is in an uncommonly finest health, and the people admire him for a state of health of his, in this age of him.

A relative of mine from Girgaon, who met me recently, told me in a casual talk that, 'I' was struck with a tragedy in the recent years, his son's wife committed a suicide for the reason unknown till now; 'I's son and wife were behind the bar and released after some days with the help of the cousin of 'I's brother in law; my relative also told that, 'I's wife has become a deranged person because of a psychological trauma she got out of a sudden incident. 'I', my relative told, has visibly become a traumatized person because of the tragedy, but his die hard habit of taking the life lightly in all the situation does not let him to get emotional and surrender to the inner feelings of his heart.

THE MADMAN

One day, a madman appeared in our lane, nobody knew where he came from, but somehow it appeared that some previous connection attracted him to our lane, or his insane mind felt some comfort in staying on in the lane. He was a lean, thin, and tall man and the insanity had brought with him all the signs, which usually any mad person betrays. He was dirty and soiled, from his top to toe; his hands, feet, neck, and larger part of the face were layered with the black dirt and the dust, his hair and beard were hap-hazardously grown and were strewn with the dust and dirt. He appeared as if he had been from a good family before the insanity grasped him. When he came to our lane, he had on him a half torn dirty shirt and the pants of the same condition. His pants were feebly holding onto his waist, and he used to pull that up, off and on, with one hand or the other. Many times, he used to disappear from the lane for several hours or, sometimes, even for two or three days, but, after having forgotten about his existence, he would reappear suddenly. In this way, he continued staying on in the lane for two to three months; sometimes, the residents of the lane might give him some leftover eatables, but he did not depend on them nor did he depend on anybody particularly, and his need of food intake was met by means of satiation in the form of say the fruits and banana vendors from the nearby *bhaji Galli* and the pedlars visiting the area.

Many days passed like that, the madman, in the meantime, had gained considerable compassion of the residents of the area, although he would not long for any emotive reflections of the people nor could he realize when they were being shown to him, for his mind had passed the stage that human emotions are sensed. His disappearances from the lane continued in the meantime. The old and obsolete clothes on his body had become more vulnerable in the meantime, and his pants, if that could be called so in that condition, would barely hold to his waist and often drop down to his knees despite his feeble attempt to maintain that in its place. He was not in a position to get obliged by the new clothes offered by the kind people, for he had lost awareness of a need to wear any other clothes than what that he had on him, which he had been thinking to be part of the body of him, like hands and feet. With the sliding of his pants every now and then, it was obvious that his secret limb would catch the eye of any man or woman.

That time, there was no system, which could take care of such insane persons on the information or complaints from the people; hence nobody was aware of what that exactly could be done in the alleviation of the miseries of such persons. One day by 11 o clock in the morning, 'the agonized wailing' was heard in the street; anyone who heard those heart rending wailing was drawn to the balcony of the house or to the nearest spot of the happening, in an eagerness to see what was happening; their eyes caught that one rowdy person from the lane was beating the mad man hard with a long stick, which the madman was trying to avoid by the strange movements of hands, in the air; the mad man's pants slid till the ankles, though his feet were still stuck into that. That rowdy person was beating the defenceless mad man mercilessly, without heeding to his wails and screams in agony, for quite some time, thereafter, having had exhausted he threw the stick away and walked back to his shop. The crime of the madman, as it was learned later, was that he appeared before the shop-cum-residence of that person in his pants fallen up to the knees, which was too indecent an action to happen in front of the women of the family of that person as if it were done purposely by any sane man of the guts. The madman made some strange gestures for some time, without being aware of the existence of a crowd gathered around, and went to one corner of one of the buildings and sat there huddled for a long time, delivering intermittent noises of anguish and pain. Before long, he fell silent and became still, he lay there for a long time, ostensibly, having gone into the sound sleep. Though, the people of lane felt extremely sorry about a plight of a hapless destitute, they, however, could not do anything, as the madman was an insignificant person for having any remedy available, during that time, in his defiance. Evening approached and soon the night began falling, the madman was lying on the spot where he had huddled, and he was in the same position that he had taken from the afternoon. It was soon sensed by the residents of the lane that he had died. Some kind soul informed the municipality; the van came, and went after the workers loaded the dead body of madman on it. It was 10 o'clock in the night and the small crowd, mainly of the children, slowly dispersed after the van pulled out; while dispersing they could see the van disappearing in the dim, mystique, and greenish light of the street gas lamps on the road yonder. Incidentally, during that time, an awareness of the human rights had not been kindled till then, and the homicides, of such type, were eluding the attention of the law keepers.

BAA

Baa was staying in the house on the second floor of the building that we were staying. In the 60s, she was a widow of above fifty years of age. Though everybody considered her to be a widow, she had been, in fact, a keep (concubine) of a man, who had begun staying with her, in the same house, in his old age; he had died staying with her in that double room, which he had taken on the rental basis for staying together with Baa; many older people in the building had known him, and they used to say that he had been a good natured person, pursuing a small business. After his death Baa became the legal occupant of that room, out of a favour from the building owner. Baa was a Maharashtrian woman, but nobody knew how she assumed that nickname 'Baa', which was a nickname for the mother, in Gujarat. She would be called Baa by everybody, from a 5 year old child to an old man of 70. In those days, a nickname of a person would be the same for everybody in the area and nobody would call a person, 5 years older to him, uncle or aunt, as is observed in the present days.

Baa would strive to keep her manners and speaking close to the title bestowed on her. Her face used to ooze out the kindness when she talked to anybody. She was a small and feeble woman, and she always used to betray a sympathetic but mischievous smile on her face, her voice was low pitched but piercing, and her speech would be full of a concern about others.

Baa was a sole owner of the place, where she was staying; she had allowed her brother, along with his one son and a daughter, to stay with her in the house. It was not known how much helpful Baa's brother was with her as far as finance was concerned, but the likelihood of his being helpful to her was distant because his own means, it seemed, was not sufficient to support his own family, without worrying every day. The man, who had died while living with Baa, had not left anything for her except the tenancy rights of the place, which was not helpful to her to pass her future life comfortably; but, Baa overcame the situation making use of whatever was left for her. Baa began keeping a family as a subtenant in her house and receiving a monthly rent from it. The monthly rent so received was perceived to be sufficient for Baa, and in the income she was able to meet her monthly expenses, which were not a large for a widow of Baa's habits. The act of keeping a subtenant was not a legal act; the building owner, however, was a considerate man and was not taking any action against Baa, except grumble about her to the other residents, when he would come every month to collect the rent from the tenants.

Mostly, the subtenant family used to be the family of a woman kept as a concubine by a man of some means, and because of that nature of the subtenant family Baa was able to receive more than the reasonable rent, for an obvious reason, from such family; the subtenant family would consist of that woman and her two or three children from her past and present keepers, the subtenant family would live peacefully in the building and establish the workable relations with the other residents of the building. The children of the building had no qualm in befriending with the children of the subtenant family of Baa, but the parents would frown if they came home. It used to happen so that the father of the earlier child of that woman, sometime, would come calling the child's name from the lane, the child would be sent down to meet his father and bring some money or gifts from him, but the manifestation of the fatherly love was allowed to take place only on the street without any consent of entering the building, for that woman would allow only her current keeper to enter her home; the earlier keepers would have been left long ago after their financial situation had become weak and they had been barely able to support any other family than their own. When the father came and called the son, shouting his name, in the lane to meet him and to give him the gifts, the naughty boys in the lane would find out slyly the first name of the father, and, after some days, they would begin calling that child by the name of his father, stealthily, from the corner of the lane. Any such subtenant family used to stay with Baa for a few years, and, thereafter, they would leave the house for the reasons unknown to anybody. A new family, maybe with a little different composition, would soon appear in the place of an earlier one, which had left.

Baa had one daughter, who was in her late twenties at the time of the early 60s. The daughter of Baa was not staying with her, she was staying at some distant place, and she came exceedingly rare to meet her mother, bringing along a big group of ladies like her; it was known that she also was kept as a concubine by some man, and, therefore, she was staying away and coming surprisingly occasionally to meet Baa.

Nobody knew the exact reasons, but the little children of the building were afraid of Baa, the mothers from the building would take their child to Baa or call Baa home if any child, mostly a boy, became an obstinate and remained unmanageable for a long time. The scolding of Baa in her peculiar piercing voice would amend the boy in no time, and if that did not work, because the boy turned out to be difficult to handle on the occasion, then Baa would take him forcibly, with the help of ever eager bigger children around, to her home and tie him to the railing of the gallery until the boy surrendered unconditionally and gave a promise for the good behaviour in the future. Scarcely the boy regained his senses when Baa would return to her composure, wipe off the teary face of the child with the corner of her sari, offer him some sweets or toffee, and reach him home telling the mother that, her son was now a lovely boy, and also instructing her for giving the boy a thing, for which he was stubborn and behaved badly at a time, when he would do well in his next examination. The people of the building had seen many children, much bigger in size and taller in height than Baa, shivering in their half pants when they were made to stand before Baa for receiving her scolding. In that way, an intermittent or sudden issuance of a verbal certificate from Baa, of a boy being an obedient and wise, would send a boy into an ecstatic pleasure. It was heard that the fathers from the building were sometimes advising their wives to entrust their unruly boy to Baa for his essential mending.

Baa's native place was in Goa, but she was never seen going to her native place, moreover, nobody was ever spotted coming to see her from her native place, except her brother and his children already staying in her home; mother of the brother's children, however, would sometimes come from the native place and stay for some months.

The religious events in the home of Baa would be different from that in the other homes; sometimes, some *Pooja* would be done that only ladies would participate, sometimes, Baa would be found visiting the threshold of every home in the building and begging for the alms, for that would have been her vow before the god that she would beg home to home and raise the expenses of *Pooja*; actually the vow was required to be fulfilled only as a formality, but Baa would be found fulfilling vow seriously.

The children in the building, in the 60s and the 70s, remember Baa not only for their 'pissing in the pants' condition, when they had an occasion to stand in front of her for receiving her scolding, but also for small excursions to *Chowpaty*, under her auspices, on the early nights of the spring, and the late monsoon seasons. In the months of October, November, and also February, and March, Baa, on some days would announce her intention of after dinner outing to *Chowpaty*; she would take all children, those willing children of the willing parents, under her control before an errand began. The children, under the guidance and instructions of Baa, would begin the excursion, by 8.30, after the dinner; they would first proceed toward Prarthana Samaj and, from there, take a left turn to reach the bridge, which lies opposite the Roxy Theatre and goes over the railway track and the Marine Drive, after crossing the bridge they would reach on the promenade, near the swimming pool, by the side of the sea, after walking a few steps on the right they would reach the massive sand bed of *Chowpaty* (the seashore). The group would settle and sit in the circle, on the sand bed of the sea, after selecting a suitable place. *Chowpaty,* in those days, was not a crowded place as it is today; the sight of the neon signs visible from the distant spots, in the otherwise dark surroundings; an invigorating and salty breeze slowly coming from the sea; the shimmering lights on the ships, in the distant sea; and the coolness of the massive sand bed would send everyone into an ecstatic world. In the delighted state of mind, the group would begin chitchatting on some petty issue like cinemas, heroes-heroines of that time, cine magazines, sports and besides, but excepting the subject of studies; some girls would begin singing a song on the slightest insistence, someone would suggest the game of song riddles and the suggestion would just be upheld and implemented, the boys would start playing in the sand, in the nearby area, in the sight of Baa, some grown boys would go to mysterious area as far as the deserted limits of *Chowpaty* and present some information of interest. The *ganderiwalas* (the sellers of the pieces of peeled sugar cane) and the *shengwalas* (the sellers of the ground nuts boiled in salted water) would be hovering around the group, the boys and girls would contribute and get the *ganderis* and the *shengas*, which would be eaten by everybody, under the kindly direction of Baa, in a due proportion; sometimes, Baa would contribute a bigger sum toward the expenses, and, sometimes, she would not be allowed to contribute by the children. The calls, in the style of Johnny Walker (an actor—from 'Pyasa' picture), of the *champi-malishwalas* (the masseurs) would be heard from the distance, but they would not come nearly as they had no hopes of finding any customer in a group of children.

When the minds of the children were refreshed to the fullest then Baa would suggest preparing for going back home, the place would be left after having spent more than one and half hours there; everybody would gather together and begin the journey homeward, with Baa giving particular attention to the girls and the little boys. They would take the similar way that they had come; very rarely Baa would give in to the suggestion, from the grown up boys, of taking a different route, which was a little risky to undertake for a group of the children, for that route required the crossing, in the speeding traffic of Marine Drive, at one point. That route was like—to walk on the promenade, till opposite the Charni Road station, then cross Marine Drive to reach the bridge over the Charni Road station, cross the bridge to land in Kele *Wadi*, pass Kele *Wadi*, and there came the building, where the homes were. Baa would be more careful in leading the children back home than what she had been whilst taking them to the *Chowpaty*, as by the time they returned the roads would have become more lonely and more quiet, giving an indication of the approaching midnight. The time when all reached home would not be beyond 11 o'clock and the people at home should be in a readiness to go to sleep, the boys and girls returned home in time would relieve the parents of any worry, although, they would not be worrying much when the children had gone with Baa. The memories of the late hours spent on *Chowpaty* must still be lingering in the hearts of many, who have shifted to another house several years since, and who are now in their 60s.

Most of the buildings of Girgaon were constructed after the technique of load bearing, and they were more than 40 to 50 years old in the 60s and the 70s. Any heavy activity on the upper floor would make some dry earth or soil spilling in the rooms below. Baa was staying just below our house, and her hall and bedroom were similar to our house from wall to wall; any jumping, thumping, shifting, or dragging of heavy furniture on the floor of our house would make the dry soil fall in her rooms. If such things happened in our house and the dry soil began falling in the Baa's room, Baa would be shouting from her window, for us to learn, that, 'mind well, human beings and not the animals are staying below'; that warning would prompt us to wind up the activities or to go to Baa for explaining her and requesting her to stand with the inconvenience for some time. If any boy in our house took to jumping and, in a trance like mind-set gained at a time with him, remained unheeded to the warnings delivered by Baa from her window, then, at length, Baa would appear at our door and catch the culprit boy red handed; my mother would come from the kitchen and instead of Baa complaining to her my mother would complain to Baa about a heedless attitude of the delinquent boy, both of them would pull the ears of the boy and warn him against any rough behaviour in the future.

A year after a year passed and then passed many years; the subtenants in the Baa's house came and went. By the mid-70s, the creed of women, that Baa used to find her subtenants giving a hefty rent, began thinning in size, as many women of that creed began perceiving emptiness in remaining some man's concubine, and the men of means, who could keep them and support them, also became scanty in numbers, in the changing times. Baa reconciled to the changing circumstances and began keeping homely families as a subtenant, who of course had no reason to pay more than a reasonable amount of rent to Baa.

By the mid 80's, the Baa's daughter, who was past her prime age by then, shifted to Baa's house with an intention of staying there forever. The relations between the mother and daughter were not as warm as they are in the other families, they were quite indifferent to each other, they, however, were not seen quarrelling any time, and their interaction with each other was on a workable level. By the end of the 80s, Baa was seen walking and moving unusually slowly in the house, she would not leave the house because she had become too weak due to the old age; while going past her house, if the eyes met, she would look with a piteous face. Soon, Baa was admitted to the government hospital, where she was left lying for several days; her daughter would visit her terribly rarely, only out of a formal courtesy; as the days passed the daughter's visits to the hospital became more and more scarce; once it happened so that the daughter did not visit the mother for several days at a stretch, where after on one afternoon a ward-boy from the hospital came searching the house of Baa, he informed that, Baa had died twenty four hours since, and, that, he had been sent to give the information at home as no person knowing Baa was around her at the time of her death, and the long-time thereafter.

*   *   *